'*Ordinary Miracles* is an hon~ ~ ~nd
thought-provoking read. Ch  ic
narrator, sharing the highs an is
family and friends have been 'e
established a vibrant Chur ~r
Manchester. The result is a fait~ ~~~~~~~
Mike Pilavachi, Director, Soul Survivor

'We're often drawn to the people who tell us to "dream bigger".
Here is a book that will provoke you to "dream smaller" – and I
guarantee it will set your heart on fire. I know Chris well. He has
the authority of a prophet, theologian, activist and that great guy
in the noisy house down the road. With his family, they are
practising the art of staying put and seeing God build His
kingdom through the mess, meals and mundane moments of life.
Don't read it if you want to escape into the fantasy that God will
only use you if you're in the perfect job, perfect house or perfect
church. Jesus has moved into the neighbourhood and is staying
put. Question is, will we?'
*Rachel Gardner, Founder of Romance Academy; President, Girls'
Brigade E&W; Trustee, Home for Good; Volunteer Youthworker*

'This is an honest, passionate account of an ordinary man in an
ordinary church attempting extraordinary things in Jesus' name.
I can be so certain of this because I've known Chris for nearly 30
years – man and boy and church leader. To all who want to join
in the adventure of mission, this book will inspire you, make you
laugh, and give you hope that God does really wonderful things
in unexpected places.'
Dr Neil Hudson, Salford Elim Pastor; Church Consultant, LICC

'I read this book because I esteem Chris Lane; as a friend, teacher,
theologian and church leader. So will you when you finish this.
This book is honest and inspiring, authentic and challenging. I
love Chris' compelling case for the centrality of the table, costly

living, commitment and the challenge to all too normative ideologies in church culture. But its real strength is in the responses it will draw out from us. Not to be impressed with Chris or Langworthy – but to be more committed to Christ and the local church He has called each of us to. Put that other book down and buy this one instead.'

Rev Canon Chris Russell, Vicar, St Laurence Reading; Advisor to the Archbishop of Canterbury

'This book is fresh, gritty, laugh-out-loud and full of hope. Chris Lane offers a feast of theologically rich reflections from his eighteen years church planting on the Langworthy Estate in Salford. It's about "ordinary miracles. If you blink you might miss them. Keep your eyes open, and you see them everywhere". May this book inspire you to watch & pray for the miracles Jesus loves to do today – in ordinary places, often around a table, with the unlikeliest guests. If you're hungry – come to the banquet. May there be Fire in urban estates across the North West and beyond!'

Rev Dr Jill Duff, Director of St Mellitus College, North West

'It's been said that by reading we live many lives. This is the chance to "live" Chris' adventure of obedience. It's an opportunity to discover what being out of your comfort zone feels and smells like. It's full of joy, heartache and faithfulness. It's human and normal, a story we can all relate to. Yet at the same time it's full of transformation that only God could be behind. An inspiring read – I recommend it!'

Andy Croft, Associate Director, Soul Survivor

ORDINARY MIRACLES

MESS, MEALS AND MEETING JESUS IN UNEXPECTED PLACES

Chris Lane

instant
ap[]stle

First published in Great Britain in 2017

Instant Apostle
The Barn
1 Watford House Lane
Watford
Herts
WD17 1BJ

Every effort has been made to seek permission to use copyright material reproduced in this book. The publisher apologises for those cases where permission might not have been sought and, if notified, will formally seek permission at the earliest opportunity.

The views and opinions expressed in this work are those of the author and do not necessarily reflect the views and opinions of the publisher.

British Library Cataloguing-in-Publication Data

A catalogue record for this book is available from the British Library

This book and all other Instant Apostle books are available from Instant Apostle:

Website: www.instantapostle.com
E-mail: info@instantapostle.com

ISBN 978-1-909728-76-9

Printed in Great Britain

Acknowledgements

Esther: we've always done this together, and you've always been up for an adventure. My finest achievement in life was persuading you to marry me! I genuinely don't know what I would do without you. Maybe I might buy a hamster.

Daniel: sportsman, baker, drummer. Rebekah: runner, reader, cuddler. Hannah: comedian, leader, character. I couldn't be more proud of the three of you.

Mum and Dad: you cheered us on and supported us throughout this whole crazy adventure, and taught me how to follow Jesus. You are my role models.

Ar Kid: you're my best mate, and you and Natalie demonstrate with your lives what following Jesus is all about. And of course, you are a true giant of urban ministry.

Gill and Rafael, Joan and Nick, Ruth and Tom, Barbara and Patrick, Gwen: you have meant so much to us and been so generous and kind to us. Thank you.

My Langworthy Community Church family past and present: this is not my story, but ours. You have chosen this path when you could have been elsewhere, and together we have seen the beauty of God's kingdom in our life together. And we are just getting started! We will carry on eating, welcoming, praying, loving, and playing Kubb.

Andrew and Beth: you are true friends. What a joy it is to lead with you both, and learn so much from you, as well as the many other legends in LCC who make all this happen.

Mike Pilavachi and our Soul Survivor family: Mike, thanks for being an amazing friend and consistent support for so many years, and for providing a spiritual home for us with Soul Survivor.

Andrew Belfield: you've been a constant support, a wise advisor and a dear friend.

Paul and Nicky Hutchings: you lived this out with us over so many years and taught me loads.

Andy Hawthorne and The Message: without you guys, your vision and incredible generosity to us, this wouldn't have happened. Thank you.

Mount Chapel: for your kindness to us and commitment to the gospel and for everything I learned from you all in the course of twenty-six years.

To all who were so kind as to read through the manuscript and offer comments and some endorsements – you have all been a great support to me: Mike, Andy Croft, Graham Cray, Chris Russell, Marijke Hoek, Jill Duff, Malcolm and Joyce Lane, Neil Hudson. Thank you.

Manoj and all at Instant Apostle for taking a risk on me to publish our story.

To all who have supported us in prayer, finance and friendship over the years: thank you.

Contents

Foreword

One of the greatest challenges facing the Church in these multicultural, multi-faith and, in many places, post-Christian times is how to draw to faith people with no church connection or interest in a connection. In addition, Christian ministry in poor urban communities remains as challenging as ever. The 'obvious' irrelevance of the Church in many people's perception is a far greater obstacle to mission than hostility. There is no simplistic, one-size-fits-all answer. I have long been convinced that one aspect of the answer lies in planting new culturally appropriate churches, in going to these communities and networks, rather than inviting people to a reworked version of what is already there in an existing church! There is a movement of the Spirit which involves going to communities which are disconnected, and discerning how a Christian community which serves the kingdom of God for that local community could take shape. The work in which I have been involved calls these 'Fresh Expressions of Church', but the label is not important.

The story my friend Chris tells in *Ordinary Miracles* is a fine example of participation in this initiative of the missionary Spirit: an eighteen-year-long obedient response to the call of God for a very challenging task: planting a church for those who don't like church, and doing it in a poor urban community.

Every context is different, but there are principles here which are appropriate for many contexts. They have been learned the hard way, in a journey from missionary innocence to proven experience. Wisdom and appropriate praxis were learned along the way.

They include the importance of patient incarnational ministry, of commitment to the long-term well-being of a place, focused on the transformation the kingdom brings, rather than on immediate numerical growth. They include an openness to the supernatural working of God without signs and wonders being treated as a short cut avoiding costly identification. They include hospitality and a culture that is non-judgemental, resulting in a different sort of 'messy' church (I like both sorts), with patience, prayer and long-term commitment offering stability to unstable lives. So many things are held together in this story that properly belong together, but are not often found together. The whole account is of an exercise in discernment, learning to join in with what Jesus is doing in the neighbourhood, rather than bringing Him to a place He has never visited before.

This an honest book, telling of the disappointments as well as breakthroughs. This sort of ministry requires vulnerability and hope. To my great delight, the journey has made Chris a practical theologian. It led him to some serious study, bringing the questions raised by his experiences in Langworthy to the Scriptures and the Christian tradition, then joining in with what Jesus was doing there, in the light of what he was learning.

Another friend recently published a book about the growth of the early Church, focusing on the virtue of patience as a key to understanding its growth.[1] Despite our twenty-first century addiction to instant answers, the reconnection of communities to the good news of Jesus Christ requires faith-filled patience. This book recounts the patient ferment of the church in Langworthy. I recommend it warmly.

Bishop Graham Cray (formerly leader of the Fresh Expressions Team, chair of the Soul Survivor Trust)

---

[1] Alan Kreider, *The Patient Ferment of the Early Church* (Grand Rapids, MI: Baker Academic, 2016).

Introduction

It was a Saturday lunchtime on a rainy May weekend away in mid Wales. In the log cabin canteen, seventy-five of us gathered around the tables, talking, laughing and tucking into the fish (slightly dry) and chips (occasionally overdone but generally OK). For a church group, we were a strangely eclectic bunch. Looking around the room, there were two self-professed atheists, a Muslim, and probably twenty others who would not have described themselves as Christians. On one table there was a lady who had arrived so drunk the night before that she couldn't put her young daughter to bed, sitting next to two of our prayer team and a guy in the second year of his PhD in Church history.

As we got ready for dessert, I introduced the group to Brian, who had been volunteered to tell his story. A stocky, shaven-headed Mancunian covered in tattoos, he was nervous speaking to a group of this size and had written his story out word for word. He proceeded to read.

'For most of my life I was an alcoholic and a drug addict. I tried all kinds of techniques to stop. When I got married I stopped for a while for my wife, but it didn't last long. Then when I had kids I tried to stop but failed then too. I've been in and out of prison, rehabs and mental hospitals, but always went back to the drink and drugs. A guy told me,

"Only God can help you, Brian." I said, "I am God – I make my own decisions."'

He continued, 'But then one day I got so desperate that I got down on my knees and said, "God, if you're real, I need You to help me."' Then he looked up from his paper, shaking with nerves, and scanned the room. 'It's been seven years since that day, and in all that time I've never touched a drink or a drug. The only explanation I can come up with is that God saved me on that day – it was a miracle.'

At that moment, there was a brief silence as we took in his words and then, almost as one, the whole room stood to their feet and started clapping and cheering. I remember looking at some of them and thinking, 'Why are you clapping? You don't even believe in God!' As we stood together that day, there was a strange yet tangible sense that Someone else was standing with us, that we weren't just clapping a great story but the One behind that story. It was a holy moment. The Risen Jesus was with us around the table, just as He had been with His first followers at Emmaus, or at the beachside barbecue. In that moment, Jesus unified our ragtag group together as all of us recognised Him in a story, and we dared to hope that if He could do that for Brian, He could transform a whole estate.

I have opened with this story because in many ways it captures the essence of the story I want to tell in this book. At one level it is the story of a group of friends planting a church in an inner-city estate known for serious deprivation and crime. But it is not just for those interested in church planting in the inner city. It is an attempt to describe how hope and beauty and healing can be found in the darkest and most desperate of situations. It is a story of mess, miracles and meals. Of the most unlikely people finding themselves welcomed into the life of Jesus' kingdom, eating at His table and inviting others along.

I hope you will find our stories encouraging, and perhaps you will be challenged at times too. I have tried to convey a sense of what we have learned in the course of eighteen years living in and loving one place – the Langworthy estate in Salford. I have also attempted to pass on some of what I have learned while writing an MA dissertation on Jesus' meal table – one of the central features of Jesus' life, message and ministry – and how we as a church have tried to live out the radical inclusivity of Jesus' table in our own context. Jesus broke the social and religious conventions of His day and caused outrage by eating with sinners and tax collectors, and welcoming the outcasts into the kingdom of God.

Chapter 1
Calling

In the 1960s, when my mum was doing her teaching practice at Langworthy Road Primary School, the sprawling network of red-brick terraced housing known as Langworthy was a desirable place to live. It was a proud working-class area where doorsteps were cleaned every day and you could leave your back door open, and everyone knew you and looked out for each other.

By the late 1980s, when I was making the big leap to high school, that had all changed. Sometimes a rumour would go round school that the 'Langworthy Lads' were waiting at the gate for a fight, and the whole school would leave by one of the other gates. I lived a mile away from Langworthy, but it was a different world. I would never walk down into the estate on my own. In those days if you lived in the estate it was difficult to get tradesmen to come to your house, as most refused to come owing to the risk of theft or violence from the gangs.

In the early 1990s, around a third of housing in Langworthy was unoccupied, with windows boarded up owing to the mass exodus of many of the residents who could no longer cope with living there. The church I attended from childhood, a church with Brethren roots which had experienced a charismatic renewal, was situated at the top of the Langworthy estate. Mount Chapel was a kind of 'city on a hill', with windows looking out over the estate, with some congregation members who had lived in Langworthy during the good times, and one or two who were trying to survive there still.

It was around this time when we started to pray consistently for the estate. There were some who had done this for years, but a weekly 6am prayer meeting began to attract larger numbers and hearts were stirred to pray for change. The church opened a coffee shop on the main road, The Lighthouse, and began reaching out through that building. At the same time, the young people of the church began to experience the Holy Spirit and join in the prayer for Langworthy.

I was one of those young people. With some friends, I started gathering the youth to worship and pray together, and we began to regularly walk down into Langworthy to pray on the streets for change to come. As we continued to pray, it became clear that our outreach efforts so far were just a small beginning.

Andrew, my little brother, is four years younger than me. In Salford we call our siblings *Ar Kid*. Ar Kid is typical of little brothers – he's louder than me, more competitive and definitely more annoying. He is also my closest friend and we have worked together ever since he grew as tall as me (well, one inch shorter, actually). One day as we walked and prayed together around Langworthy, we realised that God was calling us beyond praying for the estate and giving out free cupcakes every now and again. We had to move in.

This was not the news we wanted to hear from the Lord. As we prayed for revival, we had secretly hoped that the Holy Spirit would go out under the doors of the church, down the hill like a mighty river, and do all the work for us while we prayed and worshipped. Then we would do a free car wash or give out cakes, and people would ask us how they could be saved. In fact, we used to have lots of visions of rivers flowing from the church down the hill and willow trees being planted and growing up and bringing healing to people. It's just that we hadn't thought that we might be in that river and we might be some of the trees being planted there.

A few years before, I had experienced a vision of sorts while at a conference in Canada. I saw in my mind a picture of Langworthy from above, covered in darkness. Planes flew over, dropping what looked like bombs into the darkness. Wherever they dropped, a circle of light would puncture the darkness. I sensed God saying 'these are Christians moving into the estate'. I also had the feeling that I was supposed to be one of them, but decided to put that to the back of my mind. If I ignored it for long enough, perhaps it would go away? It didn't.

We started to look for a place to live. There was plenty of choice! In the meantime, we pressed on with gathering young people from across the city to pray and worship. We went along with a group of the young people to a summer festival called Soul Survivor. I will never forget sitting in a huge cow-shed in Shepton Mallet with 5,000 other young people and having the unexpected feeling that I had come home. The intimacy in worship was wonderful, but what blew us away was the way the young people were introduced to a transforming experience of the Holy Spirit in a manner so free of hype, so seemingly ordinary, so natural and yet supernatural.

We returned to Salford that summer determined to learn all we could from our experience of Soul Survivor. Early the next year, in February 1997, I went to one of their training days with my friend James, a worship leader from our youth events in Salford. We had a naïve notion that if we could only get the people from Soul Survivor to lay hands on us and pray for us, we would somehow receive their anointing and become the amazing men of God we longed to be! Driving down the M6 and M1, everyone's favourite motorways, we didn't have a clue how significant this weekend would be.

At the end of the training day, James and I approached Mike Pilavachi, the leader of Soul Survivor, and in an embarrassed 'I'm not important but you're a famous Christian celebrity' voice, we asked if he would pray for us. To our surprise he answered, 'Yes, I've been wanting to pray for you two all day!' Now slightly apprehensive, we sat down with Mike on a sofa at the back of the warehouse.

He began to prophesy to us both. Unexpectedly and to my great embarrassment, I starting crying uncontrollably. I wasn't into such shows of public emotion. Mike said to us, 'God is calling you guys to work together, a pastor and a worship leader, and you're going to minister together over the next few years, and you're going to have a really close friendship like that of David and Jonathan in the Bible.' After a few other words he turned to me and said, 'I might be wrong here, but I think God is saying you're going to be a church planter.'

By this stage I had composed myself and started to write down everything that had been said. Mike encouraged us to keep in touch and said he would support us in any way he could. He has kept his word ever since.

Travelling home to Salford we went over what had been said. It was amazing how Mike had never met us and yet referred to us as pastor and worship leader. He had also quoted three verses we had been discussing that weekend. As for the thing about church planting, I hadn't thought about it before and couldn't think of why I would ever need to, but perhaps he hadn't got everything right. Put it in the prophecy folder and come back to it in a few years!

The next day we went to our home church in the evening. I was next to James again and our youth leader, Rob, came to pray for James. I listened in and heard Rob say, 'This is strange, James, but I think God is saying you're like Jonathan in the Bible.' I looked straight at Rob and he looked round and said to me, 'And you're David. And God is saying that you two are going to have a close friendship over the next few years as you minister together. And Chris, I think God is saying that you're going to plant a church in Langworthy.'

So that was unexpected.

In the next two months, two other people said the same things to us. All people who didn't know each other, or hadn't heard what had been said. Perhaps God might be trying to say something to us? Looking back at that time now, it was an extraordinary sequence of events, and not something I have experienced before or since. It would be another seven years before we would actually plant a church in Langworthy, but those words were precious to us when we doubted ourselves, or when things got tough. God knew the task ahead and gave us courage and hope.

Andrew and I continued to look for a place to live in Langworthy, and were now joined by James. He was a southerner from Cheltenham who had come to Salford to study, and now found himself sensing a call to move into Langworthy. As James led us in worship we would usually end up in prayer and intercession for the estate, on our knees, singing, praying and prophesying words from the prophet Isaiah. Ancient words written two and a half millennia ago in the Middle East began to express what we sensed God was speaking to us about this forgotten place in the north-west of England:

> O afflicted city, lashed by storms and not comforted, I will build you … great will be your children's peace … you will have nothing to fear … Terror will be far removed.
> *Isaiah 54:11-14*

> Arise, shine, for your light has come, and the glory of the LORD rises upon you. See, darkness covers the earth and thick darkness is over the peoples, but the LORD rises upon you and his glory appears over you.
> *Isaiah 60:1-2*

As we walked down half-empty streets full of graffiti-covered boarded-up windows and shattered glass, we would read out the words of the prophet: 'No longer will they call you Deserted, or name your land Desolate.' We imagined ourselves as the watchmen on the walls who were called to 'give yourselves no rest, and give him no rest' until we saw this place turned around (Isaiah 62:4,6-7).

'Is that Chris Lane? Andy Hawthorne here. Mike Pilavachi and Pete Greig have both told me that you and I need to meet up – can we arrange a time?' I had heard Andy's gruff voice before, but only on the stage at big events talking about the amazing work of The Message, an organisation reaching into schools across Greater Manchester with their high-energy evangelistic band, The World Wide Message Tribe. We had continued our friendship with Mike at Soul Survivor, and also got to know Pete Greig, who would eventually start the 24–7 prayer movement. Both of them had mentioned us to Andy as potential local partners in the city region of Greater Manchester.

We sat round a table in The Message office, which at the time was not so much an office, more of a section of a church hall separated off by a curtain! As well as Ar Kid, myself and Andy, there was a guy called Cameron Dante, a Salford-born DJ and rapper who had recently come to faith and added his considerable talent to the Message Tribe.

I enthusiastically launched into an explanation of all we were doing in Salford: the monthly worship events called Heat that were attracting more than 200 young people from across the city and beyond; the work with our church young people and how they were encountering the Holy Spirit, reaching out to their friends and some as young as 14 were preaching and leading with us; the Heat worship band that had been formed for the meetings and was now travelling around the UK to lead worship at events and conferences.

Andy didn't look too impressed. In fact, I wondered if he was bored. He was looking round the room, as if searching for a way to escape. Almost as an afterthought, I mentioned that Andrew, James and I were looking for a house and had felt God calling us to move into Langworthy to live and work there for the next few years. Suddenly Andy made eye contact – a kind of urgent and excited eye contact – and leaned forward.

'We've just started this thing called Eden in Wythenshawe. We moved thirty youth workers into this estate called Benchill – to live in the estate for at least five years – not just to do mission there for a week and then retreat back to their nice middle-class suburbs, but to commit their lives to that community and the young people who live there. I thought it would just be that one project, but a friend has just prophesied to me that we will have ten Edens across Greater Manchester. What if we work together to plant our next Eden in Langworthy, and instead of just the three of you moving in, we can recruit twenty-five others too?'

Another unexpected occurrence.

And so it was that, between April and September 1999, James, Andrew and I moved into Langworthy, along with twenty-five others from all over the country and even one guy who moved all the way from Australia! We were told by one estate agent that they didn't understand why anyone would want to move in there, didn't think we should, and gave us an envelope full of keys to show ourselves round, as they refused to come! For those with enough money to buy, a three-bedroom three-storey terraced property would cost you less than £5,000. There was a rumour that another estate agent was running a buy-one-get-one free offer on their properties in Langworthy!

As it worked out, all twenty-eight Eden workers rented or bought houses on four streets, so that from every house you could look out of the window and see another Eden property. This gave the team, many of whom were just eighteen and had never lived away from home before, a sense of security. It wasn't rare to see young people jumping up and down on a car roof while their parents looked on, laughing. I lived opposite a drug dealer who knew more young people than the whole of our Eden team! One day I arrived home to find our front door lying on the sofa. Every room had been ransacked but nothing stolen. They had mistaken our house for the dealer's, and the only drugs they could find were a couple of packets of paracetamol. I was slightly offended they hadn't taken any of our stuff!

The atmosphere in the estate in those days was lawless. For two months either side of Bonfire Night you would often see children shooting fireworks out of drainpipes down the street towards passers-by, or posting them through letterboxes. I once watched a van being rammed into a front door to break it down, and a woman upstairs screaming. I actually thought twice about calling the police: 'What if they find out it was me and come for me?' I did call the police, but the fact I had to consider it shows how people were kept in fear at the time.

After a year of living in Langworthy, The Message converted the old church coffee shop in the heart of the estate into a state-of-the-art youth centre for the team to use as a base. It was called, and still is called today, the LifeCentre. Members of the community helpfully told us, 'It'll be burned down within six months.'

As the months turned into years, team members came and left. Some found the area too difficult to cope with; others moved on to new jobs or finished university and entered new phases of life. Too many reached a kind of burnout – disillusioned, cynical, tired, or a combination of all three. A project as radical as Eden promised much in terms of excitement, adventure and imminent revival, but often the young recruits were unprepared for the pressures of simply existing in a place ruled by fear and lawlessness. Looking back, a project aimed at being there for the long term should have demanded less and promised less, and invested, pastored, prayed and rested more – particularly in the early days.

This is not to say that all was doom and gloom, of course. We saw young people meet God in wonderful ways, and some of their stories will be told as this story unfolds. Some of the original team are still living in the area today, and are thriving. Others have moved on to do similar things in other areas. During the most difficult times there was often a wonderful sense of community and support.

On a personal note, I was one of the people who came close to burning out. Being part of the Eden leadership as well as being heavily involved in leading the youth work in church, running the Heat meetings and being part of the Heat band travelling round the country while living in a difficult area in the first months and years of marriage –

Esther and I were married in October 1999 – this took its toll. I knew I was called long term to this place, even to plant a church eventually, but after three years I was finding it difficult to keep going.

The relationship between my church and the Eden project was straining too, and this affected me deeply, as I felt a strong call to both and a love for a church I had attended for twenty-six years – since I was born. In 2001 The Message did a follow-up mission a year on from the amazing Soul Survivor: The Message 2000, when Soul Survivor had relocated to Manchester for ten days of mission encounters.

2K1: The Urban Adventure was all based in Langworthy and is one of my most precious memories from this time. Around 800 young people gathered for a week of mission to our estate, and in our local park my band, Heat, were able to lead them in worship and intercession using songs we had written for Langworthy. Friendships made in the community that week have passed the test of time.

Mike from Soul Survivor came up to speak at the mission and James, Andrew and I, together with my wife, Esther, and James' wife, Hayley, all met up in my front room one afternoon. Mike looked at us all and said, 'What's wrong? You all look terrible!' All of us had been feeling the pressure and Mike had spotted it! As we talked and prayed that afternoon, we realised that none of us were in a good place and something had to change. Mike suggested spending some time – a year or two – with them in Watford, a time to rest and reflect, to re-envision and be equipped to return. I said thanks, but no thanks. I knew I was called to Salford.

God had other ideas.

In February 2002, the five members of the Heat band moved to Watford. We had managed to persuade our bass player, John, to come with us, and he lived with us for much of that time, becoming my brother from another mother. Esther and I would be there for exactly two years, much to our surprise. Our time there was all we hoped for and more – restful, equipping, re-envisioning, restoring our passion for Jesus and our heart for mission. We enjoyed it so much that after a year of being there, when one friend called me to ask when I was coming back to plant a church, I said, 'Well, I'm quite enjoying it here now, the southerners are quite friendly!'

Esther and I knew that God wanted us back. Our great friends James and Hayley would move on to other places and callings, but Salford was calling us home. Sadly, the relationship between my home church and the Eden project had reached breaking point. I arranged a meeting with the leaders of the church, where I shared my vision to see a new expression of church planted for the people of Langworthy. Not something to rival the other churches, but to seek to reach those who no one else was currently reaching. I also shared the prophetic words about church planting that I had been given.

It had been a really difficult time for all involved, especially during the time I was in Watford, but the leaders of Mount Chapel were incredibly gracious and prayed for me and released me, Esther and the remaining twelve members of the Eden team to plant a new church in the heart of our estate. And so it was that in February 2004, Esther and I returned from southern exile into our Promised Land.

We began with a team of wonderful people who were quite tired, too busy but hugely committed. Ar Kid was still there, known and loved by almost every young person in the estate. He had missed out on the Watford adventure to pursue a woman, who was now his wife. Natalie had moved up from Croydon to dance with The Tribe, and joined the Eden team, and they became a fantastic evangelistic team working across the schools of Salford.

The new Eden team leader, Paul, and the LifeCentre manager, Nicky, another husband-and-wife team, formed the original core leadership of the church with Esther and I. Paul and Nicky had made the national news when they had relocated to Langworthy from Portsmouth in late 1999. The headline 'Can this couple increase the value of your house?' accompanied an article attempting to explain the Eden phenomenon of young professional Christians relocating to the forgotten areas of Greater Manchester. Paul was a quiet, entrepreneurial guy, full of ideas and constantly doing all the unseen things, and Nicky a great communicator, visionary and supremely well-organised and wise. Together they were an incredible blessing to me and the whole team as we set out into the unknown.

The team had a sheet with a list of expectations for every Eden team member. This included attending church and small groups, doing two to three nights of youth work a week, and weekly prayer meetings, among other things. It was well-intentioned and may have been useful originally, but it had become a burden. We ripped it up in front of everyone. We also stopped, or at least paused, a significant number of the regular outreach activities. We explained to the team that the only expectation now was to pray, and to listen together to God as He told us what to do next. After five years of living and working in this place, God had called us together not just as a mission team, but as a church.

As we got on our knees again in prayer, God began to remind the team of dreams and visions they had been given years before, but had been forgotten in the busyness of the last few years. We discovered space for friendships rather than just projects and programmes, friendships not just with each other but with our neighbours who didn't know Jesus. As we slowed down, we were more able to open our eyes to see what God was doing among us. With less noise, we could hear the gentle whisper of the Spirit more clearly. We could also hear each other, and listen to our community.

One of the difficulties we had discovered as Mount Chapel incorporated the Eden vision was that of bringing two quite different cultures together. An established church has certain ways of doing things, doesn't tend to move quickly and doesn't always cope well with change. Mount Chapel was a fantastic church – wonderful worship, quality Bible teaching, a sense of hospitality and community – but even in that there was a struggle. As the Eden team brought in young people to the meetings who would be disruptive, this was difficult both for the congregation whose meetings were being spoilt, and for the young people who sometimes felt judged and as if they didn't fit in.

I remember the times during those years when I really had a glimpse of what could be. It was not in the worship meetings but in the bring-and-share lunches afterwards. As the church relaxed and sat around tables and ate great food, something beautiful happened. The young people who had struggled to sit still in the meetings shared a table with the elderly couple who were tutting at their giggling and constant cigarette breaks during the meeting. And a connection was made. The elderly couple changed roles – from disapproving authority figures to the loving grandparents that those young people were crying out for. The young people changed roles – from silly trouble-causers to friendly kids who just wanted to be loved and heard.

It happened around *the table*. And I became convinced that if we were going to reach a whole community with the love of Jesus, it would be around a table. This is actually what Jesus did. He used the table as the place where he demonstrated what the kingdom was. The table was the place where all kinds of ragamuffins came together and found love, acceptance and transformation. The table was the place of healing and wholeness, where the most despised became the most honoured guests.

That was what Jesus was calling us to, even if we didn't have those kind of words to express it at the time – just a gut feeling and a memory of some bring-and-share lunches. Easter Sunday was approaching, so we decided that our first Sunday gathering as a church would be a meal to celebrate Easter. We hired the community wing of our local primary school, and started to invite some of the friends, neighbours and young people we had met in the previous few years to come to our Easter meal.

Our great church planting adventure had begun.

Chapter 2
Joining in with God's Mission

Our Easter meal in 2004 would mark five years since we had first moved into Langworthy. During those five years we had learned a number of lessons, one of which was a bit of theology that shaped our approach to mission in major ways. As the team had prepared to move in, most of us relocating from much more affluent areas, we were fairly young and naïve. Some of us imagined ourselves taking the light of Jesus into this dark place – being His hands and feet in a godless estate. Perhaps at times we fell into the trap of being the shiny, happy Christians coming to help these poor, disadvantaged locals – coming to teach them how to live, sorting out their mess for them. It was as if we were taking Jesus with us into a place He hadn't been before!

Gradually, we came to a stunning realisation: Jesus was already in Langworthy! Not only was He in Langworthy, but He hadn't just been waiting for us to move in, He was already at work in people's lives, bringing about His kingdom in all kinds of ways. Instead of us taking Jesus into the estate, He was already there, calling us to move in and join in with what He was doing.

The theology behind this is the idea that God is on a mission in the world – the *missio Dei* – and He calls us to join Him. Indeed, God has been on this mission since the words 'Let there be' formed life and beauty from emptiness and darkness. God's mission led to the call of Abraham in Genesis 12, when He chose a people for Himself to be a light to the world and a blessing to all the families of the earth – to show the world how to live, love and serve each other. To bring healing to a world full of the rebellion, vengeance, murder and arrogance described in Genesis 3–11. To be a people who would work to restore the hope of Genesis 1–2. This story has helped us as a church to find our place in God's Big Story, to write our own chapter, and every part of it has encouraged and challenged us at different moments over the years.

The Bible is a story of how the descendants of Abraham try to live out this great calling, leading to moments of great beauty and liberation – the Exodus, the Jubilee programmes of social justice, the lives of godly leaders such as Deborah, Elijah and Huldah, the collection of Psalms. We are shown how even the most unlikely people can be a part of God's mission – a shepherd boy who becomes the greatest king, the son of a prostitute who saves his nation, an old-age pensioner who leads his people out of slavery, a destitute refugee who becomes part of the royal genealogy.

Running throughout these stories are recurring themes. Justice for all. Peace on earth. The equal worth of all human beings, as the image-bearers of their creator. Liberation for the poor and the oppressed. Salvation and sacrifice. Covenant and community. The land and the law.

There is also a pattern. It is a cycle established in the book of Judges, and then played out in the books of Kings and the records of the Chronicler. This cycle, this repetitive sequence of events, is bookended by the Exodus and the Exile: the greatest moment of the Hebrew Scriptures, and the ultimate disaster.

To take one example, Ehud and Shamgar ruled for eighty years of peace in Israel. When they died, we are told that 'The Israelites once again did evil in the eyes of the LORD' (Judges 4:1). This rebellion brings about disaster – just as it did for Adam and Eve, and for the people of Noah's day. The people are then oppressed for many years, and cry out to the Lord for a saviour, just as they had before Ehud's reign. So God raises up Deborah to save them. She is a warrior, a spiritual leader and a political leader all in one. She brings peace for forty years. When she dies, the cycle starts again. The refrain returns: 'Again the Israelites did evil' (Judges 6:1).

Peace – apostasy – judgement – repentance – peace … Round and round it goes through the centuries, never learning from the past, always plumbing new depths of rebellion, devising fresh ways to break the covenant. The kingdom splits into two: north and south, Israel and Judah. Then the prophets emerge, calling the people back to the promises they first made to their God, to act justly and love mercy and walk humbly (see Micah 6:8). Still the people rebel, repent, return, rebel.

The prophets warn of judgement to come – as the first humans were expelled from the garden where heaven met earth, so they would be expelled from the land God had given them, from the temple where heaven touched earth and where sins were forgiven. Still the cycle continues, and judgement comes. The glory of the Lord leaves the temple and the people are taken from their land. For a generation, the people are in exile, wondering how to sing the Lord's song by the rivers of Babylon (see Psalm 137).

But God is still on a mission. A pagan king, Cyrus, becomes the agent of their return. A pagan king is 'anointed' to play his part in the mission of God! The people return to the land, but are ruled over by successive empires – Persians, Greeks, Romans – and despite a brief period of self-rule under the Maccabees, their 'exile' continues in their own land. The people cry out again for a saviour, a Messiah. A son of David perhaps, a worshipping warrior from the town of Bethlehem? Or a new Moses to lead a new Exodus, and bring the people back to obeying the covenant (Deuteronomy 18:18)? Or will Elijah return as Malachi promised?

Jesus

The second section of the great prophetic book of Isaiah (40–55) introduces a figure known as 'the servant'. At times Isaiah appears to be the servant, but more often the servant is Israel itself, trying and failing to live up to its calling. However, on four occasions, known as the 'servant songs', a figure emerges who appears to be an individual, not Israel, and not Isaiah. The servant will represent Israel, and be all Israel should have been, and will accomplish all that Israel was called to do. Some of the rabbis saw the servant songs as describing the Messiah.

This servant will bring justice to the earth, and will not falter as his people so often did. He will be called by God from birth, and will be a light to the Gentiles, bringing salvation to the ends of the earth. And somehow, the servant will take the sins of the world upon Himself, and through His suffering, healing and peace will come.

Healing, peace, justice, sacrifice. Jesus, the preacher from Nazareth, is introduced by His cousin John as 'the Lamb of God, who takes away the sin of the world' (John 1:29). His brief yet dramatic public ministry is full of controversy and confusion. He eats with all the wrong people, heals people on the wrong days, casts out demons into pigs and escapes from crowds who want to make Him king.

In Jesus' life, He demonstrates in word and deed the full beauty of the mission of God. He embodies the mission, bringing healing to the sick, peace to the troubled, trouble to the rulers and hope to the hopeless. He loves and embraces the smelly and dirty people and gives them dignity. He offends the religious leaders. Many hope that He might raise up an army to take up swords against the oppressors, but instead He tells His followers to take up their crosses and love their enemies! He tells people that God blesses the poor and ridicules the idea of the rich entering the kingdom of God.

Jesus is the word of God prophesied by Isaiah, who goes out from the Father and 'will not return to me empty, but will accomplish what I desire' (Isaiah 55:11). He brings the mission of God to a climactic moment when He hangs on a Roman cross, and the three great powers of His time – the corrupt religious system, the Roman political machine, and the spiritual powers of evil – all converge on Him at once. His people declare that He is another failed Messiah, the Romans that He is a criminal who is now crushed, and evil has its moment of apparent victory as the sky darkens and He breathes His last. He absorbs all the world's corruption and hate, and even as He dies He is praying for His killers as He taught His followers to do.

Early Sunday morning comes the moment that changes everything. The moment that would transform a group of grieving, confused and scared Jesus-followers into a movement that would eventually cover the whole earth. It was an event so earth-shattering that the eyewitnesses and those who followed them struggled for words to describe it. The resurrection accounts seem rushed, confused, excited – not at all like a clever myth being recorded years later, but like a group of people who have witnessed and experienced something they had no paradigm for, but that they felt compelled to tell everyone about, all over the known world.

As they search for the right words and a theological framework, both the writer of John's Gospel and the apostle Paul feel the need to reach all the way back to the creation of the universe itself. John starts with 'In the beginning', and his whole Gospel is an account of a new creation – day eight of the Genesis account – as an unprecedented event happens on the earth. Paul also uses the idea of 'new creation', echoing John's conviction that Jesus' resurrection represents such a new start for humanity that it can only be compared to the original creation itself.

A new day has dawned, and a new people – a new 'breed' of human beings – are about to be unleashed in the earth. If that sounds rather dramatic, it does seem to echo the force of Paul and John's language in the New

Testament. On this first Easter weekend, evil in all its manifestations has done its worst to the one unblemished human ever to live, and has been defeated. Indeed, death itself has been dealt a killer blow.

Now the resurrected Jesus commissions a people of the new creation, to tell the world what has happened, and to spread His kingdom over the whole earth. They receive the promised Holy Spirit, who will lead them into all truth, and will lead them in this mission, going before them and empowering them for all that is to come.

God's people look both forwards and backwards. They tell the great story that climaxes with the life, death and resurrection of Jesus. And they look forward to the promise of His return, the restoration of all things, when He will be all in all, making all things new – the resurrection, of which His own resurrection was a taster and a guarantee.

But it isn't a case of telling an old story and having a nice hope for the future. The resurrected Jesus, by His Spirit, is still at work, carrying out His mission now. Luke tells us that his Gospel was about all the things Jesus *began* to do and teach (see Acts 1:1), implying that Acts and beyond is about what He *continues* to do and teach.

The role of the Church today is to join in with God's mission, Jesus' mission, in the world. He is making all things new. The Christian hope of Jesus' return to put the world to rights doesn't mean that we just sit around waiting for Him to come. Quite the opposite. It means we are to anticipate that future – to be signposts showing what it is going to be like. Like a great trailer to a film, the Church should show people what the kingdom of God looks like.

When Israel travelled around the desert for forty years (as described in the book of Numbers), they sent twelve spies into the Promised Land. Ten of them were terrified by what they saw. Two of them saw what God had planned for them – a land of milk and honey, that God was giving to them. While the ten saw the obstacles, the two saw what God was doing. They brought back a huge cluster of grapes, and *while they were in the desert, they ate the fruit of the Promised Land* – the fruit of the future.

This story from Numbers perfectly illustrates how we should see our part in God's mission. Firstly, to look past the obvious obstacles (powerful people, fortified cities) and see what God is doing ('We should go up and take possession of the land … the LORD is with us' – see Numbers 13:30; 14:9), and join in with that. Secondly, to remind people of what God has done (in this case, the events of the Exodus) and give people a taste of the future – eating the grapes – while still in the desert.

What does this look like in practice? For us in Langworthy, it changed our practice of mission, and our theology of mission. Practically, we stopped putting on our own 'sanctified' versions of what others were already doing in the community. If a local toddler group is bringing community and support to people, why start our own rival group? We could serve the existing group and recognise that God is already at work there.

Another thing we did is to stop always organising our own community events in the local park; instead, Paul and I joined the local events group to work with the whole community on events to bring people together. Through this we met people who were not Christians, but were clearly being anointed by God (as Cyrus was anointed) to bring about aspects of His kingdom in Langworthy – justice, peace and joy, as the apostle Paul described it (see Romans 14:17). We sometimes told our new friends that they were doing what Jesus wanted them to do!

This was a real release for us, and with our eyes newly opened, we began to see God at work all around the estate. We were also able to have an influence for good – instead of the Halloween event, the events team decided instead to invest in a Christmas carol service involving the local schools. We would invite Christian bands to play at the events and they would share their stories of faith with the community. We discovered that 'the common good' looks very much like the kingdom of God described in the pages of the Bible. Of course, what we could bring was that connection to Jesus, and the heart transformation that only comes from Him.

As Christians we so often do our own thing, and mission is often something we do 'to' people, or 'for' them. We set up a stage and preach 'to' people. We do a garden transformation project 'for' them. But we often neglect the most powerful word – 'with'. We came into Langworthy asking the questions, 'What can we do for you? Can we tidy the alleyways? Can we clean up your garden? Can we give you this free cake?' But a much more profound, kingdom-enhancing and Jesus-imitating question is, 'Can you help us?' Or better, 'Can we do this together?' Essentially we are asking, 'Would you like to join in the mission of God?' It's basically what Jesus did – 'Come, follow Me, I'll make you fishers of men, we'll heal the sick and eat with the sinners and cast out demons together.'

One way we have seen people come to faith is when we work with them for the common good – to see the transformation we all long for – and Jesus often meets with people as they unwittingly serve Him in this way. This is not to trick people into the kingdom, but to introduce them to the source of their passion to see change and justice in society.

God is at work in all places and at all times. I now get offended when I hear a place or a person being described as 'godless', because I think it is an offence to our God who is always reaching out, always seeking the lost, always bringing His light into the darkest places. He asks that we follow Him to those people and places.

'Watch what God does, and then you do it.' So says *The Message* paraphrase of Ephesians 5:1. Our prayer now is always, 'God, what are You doing here, and how can I join in?' It makes mission and evangelism much simpler. Not any easier, but more straightforward.

I've always considered myself to be a terrible evangelist. This may come from my eagerness as a teenager to see my mates come to faith, which led me to regularly tell them they were going to hell! This lost me a few friends along the way, and didn't win any of them for Jesus!

One friend, who was really interested in my faith but was into the occult, would have big debates with me and then cast spells on me, which was a bit annoying. I kept plugging away until eventually he caved in and left his occult ways… to become a Buddhist. That was the result of my attempts at evangelism. A couple of years later, my heart leaped when he told me he believed in Jesus, like me! I asked him to share his story, and he told me how a man had given him a copy of the Book of Mormon, and he'd prayed and God had told him it was all true! So that was the kind of evangelist I was – rubbish!

Recently we ran an Alpha course. I couldn't get anyone else to run it, so I had to do it. I imagined myself ending the course with some people taking up Hinduism for the first time, or becoming Jehovah's Witnesses! I never enjoy trying to persuade people into believing in Jesus, so I wasn't looking forward to it at all. In spite of all this, it has turned into one of the best, most enjoyable things I've done in a long time. Some have come to faith, and all participants are wanting to carry on with the group beyond the course itself. It's no exaggeration to say that every week has felt like a holy moment as we have talked and prayed together.

The reason this particular Alpha course has been so good is not down to me suddenly becoming an anointed evangelist. It's not even because of the fabulous material that Alpha provide. It is because, right from the first week, we took a bold step. We made the assumption that God was already at work in the lives of those taking part, and our role was to draw that out, and to help people tie the threads together. Instead of going in trying to persuade the group of the truths of Christianity, we presented the material and then asked people to share their experiences of Jesus from their own lives. This led to many amazing moments as the group searched their own histories and found that God had been at work in their lives all the way through. People who wouldn't yet call themselves Christians began to prophesy to each other, experiencing the wonder and fear of recognising God's presence for the first time.

This way of approaching God's mission is so releasing. It takes all the pressure off us. If God is leading us here, why should we be afraid? (If God is giving us this land, why should we fear the giants?) If my job is just to partner with Him, then I don't have to make things happen for myself. I don't have to create an awkward conversation about something this person has no interest in – I just need to love them, get to know them, and as I do so I will recognise the traces of God's work in their life. My job then is to help them to see God in there. He is the One who gave them that passion for justice. He is the One who prompted them to call that person in need, just at the right time. He is the One who has led them to have this conversation, in this room, right now. And He will always be with them.

We need have no fear if God has gone before us on our mission. Our role is to follow Him, as the two spies tried to tell the people on the edge of the Promised Land. The second lesson we learn from the story in Numbers is that our calling is also to give people a taste of the future – to eat those grapes from the Promised Land.

If there is a day coming when God will heal and renew the creation itself, as He did with Jesus' dead body, then Christians should be at the forefront of creation care and environmentalism. We should embrace the Genesis call to be wise stewards of the earth, and anticipate what God will do at the resurrection by looking after the planet He has given to us to care for. Looking back, looking forward.

We look forward to a day when Jesus will reign justly over the whole earth, and we try to anticipate that by working for justice in our day – for those experiencing injustice in our own countries, and across the world. We look forward to that day, and we look back to God's heart for justice in the Jubilee programmes in ancient Israel, and the way John the Baptist, Jesus and the apostles all lived and taught the Jubilee principles in their own time.

As the Church lives as a loving community, comforting the bereaved, providing the lonely with a family, and bringing forgiveness where there once was hatred, it acts as a signpost of what is to come in the future age. It also imitates Jesus. In a world terrified by death, the Church can bring hope that Jesus has gone before us and conquered death, and giving us the promise of life in the age to come.

When Jesus returns to eradicate evil forever, this will include all sickness. Jesus showed this in His life on earth, where healing was one of the most significant features of His ministry. We should expect miraculous healing to be a part of the life of the Church – one of those fruits of the Promised Land that we can taste while still in the desert.

I was talking about these issues with a friend as we walked along a high street, past shops and restaurants, when two tough-looking guys she knew came over to say hello. One had just been released from prison, and the other had cuts and bruises all over his knuckles from a fight the previous day. My friend asked them how they were doing, and one lad said, 'Yeah, great, I've not smoked any weed for three days, I'm doing really well.' My friend then said, 'This is my mate Chris – he's a vicar!' I am not a vicar. But I thought it might be fun to pretend, so I smiled, vicar-like, and gave a mild-mannered hello.

She then made things worse: 'Can Chris pray for you for anything?' I was thinking – praying for someone in the street? This could get embarrassing. For the lads, of course;

why would I be embarrassed…? To my horror, one of the lads asked if I could pray for his hand, as he had injured it working on a building site, and it was very weak and painful to move. I was thinking I would just offer to pray when I got home, but noticed the guy had already closed his eyes, so I grabbed his hand and closed my eyes too, to shut out my awkwardness.

As soon as I touched his hand, what felt like an electrical current started running through my arm, into my hand where I was touching his hand. I opened my eyes and he was rocking back and forth as we prayed. I used my other hand to steady him so he didn't fall, then after a few seconds he opened his eyes and looked straight at me. 'What the **** just happened then? When you touched my hand, all this warmth like electricity started going into my hand!'

I started to reply, in an embarrassingly high-pitched amazed voice, '*Did you feel that too?*'

Quickly regaining my vicar-like composure, I lowered my voice and pretended this kind of thing always happened to me, as a man of the cloth. His hand was completely healed! The pain was gone and the strength returned! My friend told him he should think about following Jesus, as Jesus had been so kind to him, and he agreed. 'Yeah, I really want to do that.'

As we walked off, I said, 'I think that was a miracle!' But it didn't feel like a miracle. Or at least, it didn't feel like how I thought a miracle should feel. It felt really awkward, and I had no faith that anything was going to happen. I had imagined that I would have become full of faith and power, and spoken to the injury, rebuking it and commanding it to be whole *in Jesus' mighty name.*

Then I started to think, maybe that's how miracles feel? Maybe Peter in the Bible said to the lame man, 'In the name of Jesus Christ of Nazareth, rise up and walk!' (Acts 3:6, ESV) but in his head there was a voice saying, 'This is never going to happen. I'm going to look ridiculous.' Then when the guy got up, he was thinking, 'Flip, it even works when Jesus isn't here! Write that one down, Luke!' Maybe it didn't happen that way, but I like to think it might have. Certainly for me, every amazing thing I've seen God do has felt awkward and embarrassing at some point!

I was surprised that God had done this. But why should I be surprised? He has called me to be a signpost for His kingdom. At that moment He was drawing that young man to Himself, and reached out through the courage of my friend and through my embarrassment to show His love to the guy, in spite of how I felt or what I was thinking. If God is on a mission and is at work at all times and in all places, why not on a busy high street? On that street on that day, we were able to taste the fruit of the Promised Land – a glimpse of God's glorious future. I could have missed it if my friend hadn't pushed me to pray for them there and then. She had her eyes open to what God was doing in their lives, and we saw a wonderful glimpse of how God's mission reaches out beyond church buildings and conferences, into the lives of those who need His healing most.

Sometimes I meet Christians who have lost their direction in life, trying to work out what God's will is for them. I tell them that God's will is for them to join in with His mission in the world. Use whatever skills you have, pursue whatever you are passionate about, and join in God's great rescue plan for the world. Is it bringing justice, peace and joy? Does it involve bringing healing – to people, families, communities, or the creation itself? Is it helping to set people free from addictions, or bringing beauty and creativity to dark and desperate places? Giving a voice to those with no voice? Do it in Jesus' name. Take Paul's advice in Colossians 3:17: 'Whatever you do, whether in word or deed, do it all in the name of the Lord Jesus, giving thanks to God the Father through him.'

At the end of 1 Corinthians 15, Paul's great chapter on resurrection and the Christian life, he concludes with this exhortation: 'Always give yourselves fully to the work of the Lord, because you know that your labour … is not in vain.' As we follow God's mission in the world, nothing we do for Him is in vain – nothing is wasted. Michael Lloyd puts it beautifully:

> So it will be with the Resurrection. All the things that we do, all the work that we do for the Kingdom, every loving act, every right choice, every sacrificial deed is going to be there, as part of that rebuilt cosmos. Nothing is going to be left behind. Nothing is going to be wasted … all that we are and all that we have done that is not incompatible with the Kingdom of God will be

there, shot through with the love and the glory of God.[2]

This is our job as the people of the new creation – to play our part in God's mission, bringing beauty, hope and healing wherever we go, showing the way towards the day when God will restore all things.

After that brief interlude, it's time to return to Langworthy, and that Easter meal in April 2004.

[2] Michael Lloyd, *Café Theology* (London: Alpha International, 2006), p 227.

Chapter 3
Mess and Miracles

It was the morning of 11th April 2004. While most churches were having their Easter morning services, we were in the kitchen of the LifeCentre, peeling potatoes and chopping vegetables to make shepherd's pie. I can still remember the nervous feeling we had that morning. Would anyone turn up? If they did come, what would they think? What kind of person would come along to have Easter Sunday dinner with a bunch of Christians in a dingy school community room? We prayed as we chopped.

Our team turned up, although some were late. Then some teenagers from our youth activities arrived, and one lad had brought his mum. My thought was, 'Well, it's worth it just for them.' Then an older couple walked in. I went to welcome them, and the lady pulled me over and whispered in a broad Salford accent, 'I'm a bit drunk, luv. But I'll be OK.' (It was only midday!) This was going to be fun!

Next, one of our friends arrived who knew a lot of people across the estate. Pretty much everyone knew her. She had, shall we say, a rather exuberant personality and smoked very heavily. She took one look around the room and loudly announced, 'There's not many people here, is there?' So she got on her phone and started calling people.

'Hey, come to the school, there's free food!' She managed to bring in five more people.

As we reached the end of the meal, I prepared to get up and talk about Easter. I'd spoken to fairly large crowds in the past, but was more nervous than ever in front of this group of thirty. The atmosphere was fairly lively, but we managed to calm people down and I began to speak. Most people listened, but a young toddler starting running round the room shouting the f-word. This was a little distracting. Then the lady who was drunk starting heckling me. It was nice heckling, though – agreeing with what I was saying. It was like a Pentecostal meeting, but with real drunkenness. And swearing.

I reached the end of my talk, and said to the group: 'If you want to come back again, we're going to do this here for the next five weeks. We will eat food and talk about Jesus. We'd love to see you again.' Well, most of them. Perhaps not the swearing toddler.

To my surprise, ten of the fifteen visitors that day returned for those next five weeks. Some are still coming to our church today, and are involved in leadership. At the end of the five weeks, we seemed to be having fun, so decided to keep going – eating food and talking about Jesus. Some of our new friends who didn't yet know Jesus started to invite their friends along, and were calling it church – even though we hadn't called it church ourselves, so as not to put people off! So Langworthy Community Church was born. It was messy, and chaotic, centred around food and Jesus, and involved drunkenness and swearing. But we'd soon sort all that out, wouldn't we?

In those early days, people looking in would ask us when we planned to do a 'normal' Sunday morning service. I think the idea they had was that we were doing the meals to get people to come along, then we could make the transition into being a proper church. Others would arrive during the meal and ask, 'When are we starting church?' I would tell them we had already started! It took a couple of years to get used to that. Thirteen years later, we still eat together and talk about Jesus every Sunday. And we do the same on other days too.

That sense of chaotic mess in those early days was something I assumed would pass with time. It hasn't. In this chapter I want to tell you some stories to illustrate how God meets us in the mess and the craziness, and how He doesn't wait until we are cleaned up and sorted. I want to make a case that this is how life should be, that we should embrace the mess and let God have His way. As a good friend of mine often says, it's neat and tidy in the graveyard, but messy in the nursery, and we would prefer the new life of the nursery every time.

In the next chapter I am going to look in detail at Jesus' meal table, and what we have learned from His eating habits. But for now it is enough to say that Jesus' table was full of the most unlikely people, and earned Jesus a reputation in His community as a glutton and a drunkard – One who ate with, and therefore associated Himself with, the worst sinners.

This helped me because occasionally I would look at the pastoral situations in our church and think, 'What have we done here? Have we become a church like Corinth where Paul had to write two long letters to correct them?' When you follow Jesus in hanging out with those people of whom others disapprove, being a church who welcomes everyone, it gets seriously messy. It is also utterly beautiful and breath-taking, at the same time as being disturbing and draining.

Let me tell you Nathan's story. We first met Nathan in the park at our Monday night football sessions. He was (and is) a top lad – gets on with everyone, keeps us all entertained, and is really servant-hearted. As we got to know him and some of the other lads, we decided to take a risk and invite three of them to come to the Soul Survivor festival one summer. We felt it was a risk because they had not been to church at this point, and we thought the intensity of the meetings, with a couple of hours of worship and teaching followed by Holy Spirit ministry, which often involved shaking, crying and shouting, might be too much for the lads.

We tried to prepare them in advance, telling them what might happen and that they wouldn't be expected to stay in the meetings if they didn't want to. To our surprise, the outcome was quite the opposite to what we had expected.

At the end of the first meeting, Mike Pilavachi stood up and got everyone to stand in silence, and said, 'We are going to ask the Holy Spirit to come and meet with us.' A hushed silence ensued, into which cut the loud voice of Nathan's brother, 'Yeah, but He's not going to come, though, is He?' We decided to wait and see.

As people across the tent began to encounter the Holy Spirit, Nathan's brother asked if he could go and walk around the tent to see what was happening. As he left, Nathan told us he'd injured his knee and it was really painful. We prayed for him, and all the pain left! Then his brother arrived back from his tour of the big top. 'Nathan, there's loads of kids my age – fourteen, fifteen – and they're crying, and falling over and stuff. They wouldn't be making that stuff up, would they?' This was his usual loud voice, in a tent full of 10,000 silent teenagers, apart from those weeping.

Nathan replied, 'Look, God's just healed me knee!' to which his brother's voice came back even louder, '*Are you b********** me?*' There were some dirty looks from the Home Counties youth leaders standing nearby.

I looked round for the other lad, Matty, and noticed he was being prayed for rather earnestly by a very keen teenage delegate. I positioned myself nearby in order to cut in if any exorcisms were attempted. At one point the prayer began to pray in tongues. My heart sank as I wondered what Matty would be thinking. When it was over, I pulled him to one side to check he was OK.

'Yeah, it was good and all that, but at one point he started talking in this weird language.' I apologised for this and prepared to explain to him about the Christian practice of praying in other languages that God can give to us. But Matty continued, 'But then after a bit, I could understand what he was saying. It was God talking to me about my future, telling me that He loved me and it was going to be OK and He'd always be with me.'

WHAT???

I didn't know what to say! My first thought was, is God allowed to do that? I'm sure when I read Wayne Grudem's *Systematic Theology*, he said that only Christians can have the gifts of the Holy Spirit! Matty had just experienced interpretation of tongues – I'd never done that myself! I felt confused and excited all at the same time. What was God doing here? The lads went on to have an amazing week, spending hours in the prayer room, and always being in the meetings during the ministry times to watch and experience all that God was doing.

As I reflected on this I began to realise that maybe God isn't that bothered about Wayne Grudem's *Systematic Theology* (although I'm sure it's a good book)! Maybe God just loves Matty, and wanted to show him how much He loved him, and decided to step outside the theological boxes we try to put Him in? Perhaps the God who brings us freedom is utterly free Himself to meet with people however He chooses?

Let's continue with Nathan's story. He started coming along to church, but didn't want to become a Christian. One day he said to me, 'Is it possible to go to church, read the Bible and pray, but still not be a Christian?'

I said, 'I guess so mate, but why don't you want to be a Christian?'

''Cos I know I'd have to change.'

Another time he told me he'd felt emotional during a time of worship, so I asked him if he thought God was trying to tell him something. He said: 'Yes, I think He's saying "let me in!"'

Eventually Nathan did let God in, and it was wonderful to see him growing in his faith and reaching out to others too. As with most of us, he has had a roller-coaster kind of faith – up and down, disorientating, sometimes full-on and sometimes slow or stopping. But it is marked by the constant presence and love of God.

A few years ago he told me a story about an experience in the pub. 'There was this guy in the pub who had a bad knee, so I said I'd pray for him. So I prayed and he got totally healed.' I said how amazing that was and how brave he was, to which he replied, 'Yeah, but I probably wouldn't have done it if I'd not had six pints first.'

I will never forget one meeting where we had a time of sharing what God had been doing in our lives. One guy got up and said, 'Right, I was proper annoyed 'cos I 'ad no money and needed £100 to pay this bill. So I prayed to God, then went and won £100 on the horses. So, thanks, God!'

It's always a risk having those open mic testimonies! I always used to imagine that miracles would happen when we got holy enough, when we prayed enough or read the Bible as much as we should. Or if we managed to work up enough faith. But what we have seen is that the miracles just happen when we take a risk. When we take some people with no experience of church to a charismatic youth festival. Even when we have drunk more than we should, or are wasting our money on gambling, maybe *even there* God will meet us. In the mess of our own lives, he will come to us.

A few of us were inspired by what God did with the lads at Soul Survivor, and wondered how we could connect others with God's healing power. We had read the stories in the Gospels and seen stuff happen in that big top in Shepton Mallet, and wondered if that kind of thing could happen in our patch, in Langworthy. Surely if it could happen here, it could happen anywhere?

We heard of some people who were going out in shopping centres and offering prayer for healing. We thought that sounded cool, so decided to try it in Salford precinct, our local collection of pound shops and rip-off moneylenders. We got permission to go there fortnightly, standing just near the post office and conveniently close to Greggs the bakers. As the time for our first session drew closer, I began to get nervous, for a number of reasons.

Firstly, I'm a Salford lad. Let's be honest, standing outside the post office inviting people to sit down and receive prayer for healing is *not* normal! It's a bit strange. What if I saw some of my old school mates? Years before I had been part of a rent-a-crowd for an outreach my old church had done in the precinct. Ar Kid was part of our drama group and acted out a sort of mime of the crucifixion story, accompanied by the song 'This Blood' by the permatanned Christian musician Carmen. As Andrew lay on the floor being beaten by Roman guards, I noticed two of his old classmates standing next to me. One of them said, 'Ee-ar, what's Lano doing lying on the floor over there with them girls beating him up?' Like a modern-day Judas, I fled into Greggs for a chicken pasty.

So I didn't want to look stupid. More than that, though, I didn't have the best track record when it came to praying for healing. A few months earlier, my wife, Esther, had a pain in her ear, so I offered to pray for her. I had enough faith to pray for a good night's sleep and hoped it would be better in the morning. She had a terrible sleep, and woke up in the morning with a severe infection in *both* ears! She looked at me and said, 'You are never praying for me again!'

Salford precinct is a place where it seems that the most poorly people in Salford all gather together, to be ill.

Together. Coughing, spluttering and sneezing over each other on their mobility scooters. And I had a track record of making people get worse when I prayed for them. I was terrified that not only would I make them worse, but some might die. No one wants to see that when you're on your way out of Greggs with your sausage roll.

In the end we decided we would give it a go and take the risk. We set out a couple of chairs for people to sit on, and gave out flyers offering healing prayer. I was pretty convinced that no one would sit down. I don't think I would have sat down if it had been me. For the first few minutes I was right. We were rebuffed by people with snot streaming down their noses, bandaged arms, using crutches, you name it.

Eventually a lady came and sat down. She suffered from serious and frequent migraines, had recurring lower back pain, and a lump in her throat that she was worried about. As the team began to pray for her, she said, 'Ooo, what's happening to me? I feel like all this tingly energy is going through my body.' We explained it might be God doing something. It could just as easily have been adrenaline, the kind of experience Derren Brown can give you, so we don't make too much of those feelings. She left feeling great, and we were encouraged too.

Two months later the same lady came to find us. She told us that since we had prayed for her, she had no more back pain, no migraines, and the lump in her throat had disappeared! That encouraged us no end. During that first session, twelve people had received prayer within the two hours, and all had really appreciated us taking the time to be with them.

On another occasion, we were having a really tough time with no one wanting prayer. It was cold and miserable, and I was wanting to pack up early and go home. I walked over to Rachel, one of our team members. Rachel had come to Salford to join the Eden project, and, despite being a Scouser, was actually a fantastic person, with an incredible gift of getting alongside people and seeing Jesus have an impact on their lives.

I asked Rachel if she felt God had been saying anything, and she said that before we arrived she'd had a picture in her mind of a woman wearing a red fleece, but hadn't yet seen anyone fitting that description. I looked over her shoulder into a café nearby, and there was the Red Fleece Woman. I was delighted because not only had God spoken, but He had spoken to Rachel so she (and not me) would have to go over and start the conversation!

'There she is, off you go, Rach,' I said in my most holy voice.

She didn't need to. Red Fleece Woman stood up and walked over, and asked us to pray for her. Rachel explained the picture she'd had that morning, and shared that she felt God wanted her not to worry, that she was worried about something to do with her sister. The lady was amazed. She explained that she had MS, and was going to visit her sister in America the next week. She was worried because the long flight always took a huge toll on her health, usually meaning she had to be in a wheelchair the whole two weeks. Rachel prayed for her.

This lady came back to see us a few weeks later. She said, 'I just wanted to say thanks. I had a wonderful trip, and I was so well I didn't even need my walking stick! And my sister was a bit poorly so I was able to look after her. Am I allowed to get done again, because I've got a really sore ear?'

Needless to say, I stayed well away from the sore ear! We went out in this way on to the precinct for more than two years, and every single time, people stopped for prayer. Every single time, people had some kind of experience of God's love for them – whether physical healing, a sense of His presence, or just appreciating the love we had shown them in Jesus' name. Every single time, it was hard work and felt awkward and I didn't really want to be there.

It seems to me that this is usually how it is with the miraculous. If we want to see God do unusual things, we must step out of our comfort zones. This will inevitably feel awkward and possibly embarrassing. But who am I to let that stop me? Who am I to deny someone the opportunity to meet with the living God, just because I feel a bit awkward?

Paul said, 'Christ's love *compels us*, because we are convinced that one died for all, and therefore all died. And he died for all, that those who live should no longer live for themselves but for him who died for them and was raised again' (2 Corinthians 5:14-15, my italics). Jesus died so that we should no longer live for ourselves – His love compels us. Our love for Jesus always translates into love for the people He created, because He is a missionary God who calls us to take His love to those who need it most.

Christ's love compelled us to pray for people at Salford precinct. Christ's love compelled us to move into Langworthy. Christ's love compels us to stay when things get tough. His love compels us to overcome our embarrassments and inadequacies, and to do the stuff of the kingdom anyway. His love gets us into all kinds of adventures. His love gives a teenager who isn't a Christian the ability to interpret a message in tongues, brings healing through a drunken man's hands, and an Alpha group is enabled to prophesy to each other before they give their lives to Jesus!

As well as healing, we have also found that miracles of provision are difficult and awkward! The year we were married was the same year we moved into Langworthy to start the Eden project. I was working in an office/warehouse and doing youth work in my spare time. Esther and I became convinced that God wanted me to give my whole time to the work in Langworthy, so the week before our wedding day I quit my job, to start 'living by faith' for my income. I put this in inverted commas because all Christians are called to live by faith in all aspects of their lives, but this phrase can be a helpful shorthand for a certain way of life.

Quitting my job just as I got married was not necessarily the best way to win over my new parents-in-law. Fortunately they are both people of great faith and were fully supportive of us, as were my family. And Esther is always up for an adventure in radical living – fortunately for me! We lived that way for five years, until Langworthy Community Church were able to start paying me for three days a week, as they do now. Those five years enabled us to learn about how God provides, especially during the two years we spent in Watford.

Living nearer to London meant that our rent was triple what we were paying in Salford, for a smaller house. We had arranged to leave Salford on a Thursday in early 2002, but on the Monday of that week we still had no house to live in! As I was leaving to go down south to look at two possible places, someone gave us £1,500 in cash! I took it with me. The first house was fine, but I was told it would be two weeks before we could move in. We only had two days. The second place was great, and I was told we could move in as soon as we had the deposit and first month's rent. The total price? £1,500. I took the bulging envelope out of my pocket and handed it to my new landlord.

I imagine the landlord probably looked at the envelope and thought, 'drug dealer'. When we arrived with all our possessions in a van on the Thursday to sign the papers and move in, we were told we had failed the credit check. He had looked at my income (around £400 per month) and the cost of the house (£750 per month) and done the maths. I looked him in the eyes and with all the faith and sincerity I could muster, I said, 'I guarantee you will get your money every month, without fail.' He looked back at me, thinking, 'drug dealer'. We signed the papers, and he got his money, every month, without fail, and we never went into the red for those two years.

Now that is a pretty good story and it's all factually true. What I haven't told you is how stressful it all was. I'm not a reckless person, neither am I a Mighty Man of God, Full of Faith and Power. Leading up to our wedding, I was thinking, what the heck am I doing? What kind of man am I not to have a regular income to provide for my wife and future family? During those weeks when we had no idea how we would pay the rent, let alone afford to buy food, I wasn't some modern-day Hudson Taylor or George Mueller, giving thanks for my breakfast even though it hadn't arrived yet! I was more likely to be found playing the super-addictive computer game Championship Manager, trying to forget about my financial worries by signing Ronaldinho for Manchester United!

But God is so kind. He always provided for us. There was one week when we needed £100 to pay a bill, and on the day it needed paying, a letter arrived with £100 in it. The letter said that the sender was going to post it a week earlier, but God had told her to wait till now! God is never late, but He never seems to be early either. I found this quite annoying! But He was teaching us to trust Him. Our experiences here would help us greatly when LCC had to raise the money to buy the LifeCentre building a few years ago. The costs involved seemed so far out of the reach of our small congregation, but we knew that with our generous God and a group of people willing to give sacrificially, anything was possible.

To conclude: God loves to do miracles in and through us. The more we step out of our comfort zones and trust Him, the more we see Him do. He will not be boxed into our theology or our systems. Just because we say a prayer in a certain way, using a formula we learned from a Christian conference, it doesn't mean it will work. God wants us to develop our own relationship with Him and not use Him as some kind of magic presence we can invoke as and when we wish. As with every part of mission, we watch first where He is leading, then follow Him.

If we are willing to be so full of His love that it compels us, as it did Paul, we must be willing to obey all He commands us, and to be prepared for things to get messy. We don't fix people, that's Jesus' job. We are there to connect them to Jesus, and play our part as He does His wonderful work in their lives. As we do all these things, we will see healings in pubs and outside Greggs, and we will experience Him providing for our needs, in wonderful ways.

Chapter 4
Jesus, Hospitality and Holiness

One theme that has run through everything we have done in the short history of our church is this: food. From that first Sunday in Easter 2004 to last week when we ate Jamaican curry, eating together has been central. We have never grown up and become a proper church with a Sunday morning service in rows. Much of our service in the community involves food too: Breakfast Group in term time, Make Lunch for kids on free school meals during the holidays, weekly food parcels for destitute asylum seekers.

We have found that sitting around a table together, rather than sitting in rows looking at the back of someone else's head, deepens our friendships and provides an easy welcome for newcomers. It provides a great challenge to our preachers too. You eat your main course, get up and speak, then sit back down for dessert, where people can ask you questions and tell you exactly what they thought of what you said! It keeps things real, there is no escape into a pulpit, as you are thinking how your words apply to the people on your table.

Meeting as church around a meal table is not a new idea. It's not a 'fresh expression of church', or 'emergent' or whatever the latest cool word is. Throughout biblical history, God's people have met around a table. Jewish festivals are so centred around food that one rabbi said you could summarise all the Jewish festivals in three brief sentences: 'They tried to kill us. We survived. Let's eat!' The annual festivals of Passover, Weeks and Booths, which celebrated great events in Jewish history, and the weekly Sabbath meals were all crucial identity-forming occasions as the great biblical narratives were retold and acted out around meal tables in Jewish communities all across the Roman Empire in Jesus' day.

Indeed, what happened at the table was crucial in defining your position in society. If you ate with people of good reputation, your reputation was enhanced. If you were invited to sit near to an esteemed host, you would bring great honour to your family. Your place in the pecking order was shown by whom you ate with, and where you sat at the table. Children would be brought up to seek the best seats at meals, so as to gain respect and honour. Eating together created a bond between the diners. Plutarch referred to the 'friend-making character of the dinner table' and the Jews believed that to betray someone you ate with was the very worst kind of betrayal.

A devout Jewish host would be careful not to invite anyone of bad reputation – sinners, those unclean, and certainly not Gentiles. Jewish writings between the two Testaments of the Christian Bible show this to be true. Jubilees 22:16 says, 'Separate thyself from the nations, And eat not with them'.[3] Sirach encourages its readers to 'Let the righteous be your dinner companions' (9:16) and

---

[3] http://www.pseudepigrapha.com/jubilees/22.htm (accessed 16th May 2017).

discourages fellowship with sinners (13:17, NRSV), and warns the readers against allowing scoundrels, strangers and sinners into their homes (11:29-34). The world of Jesus' day was obsessed with table fellowship. One writer describes the Pharisees as 'a table fellowship sect' who excluded many from their tables to protect their holiness. Another Jewish group, the Essenes, also built their identity around who ate with them and where they sat, and who didn't eat with them. The table was the dividing line of their faith.

In the Gospels there are three descriptions of Jesus starting with the phrase: 'The Son of Man came'. The first two are key to Jesus' identity and are very well known: 'The Son of Man came to seek and to save the lost' (Luke 19:10, NIV 2011); 'The Son of Man came not to be served but to serve, and to give his life as a ransom for many' (Mark 10:45, ESV).

The third description is less quoted but no less significant: 'The Son of Man came eating and drinking' (Matthew 11:19; Luke 7:34). Let me put it as clearly as I can. What Jesus did and said around the table was central to all He came to do on earth. Almost every biblical scholar who writes about Jesus' table habits concludes that they are central to His ministry. If we are to fully understand how the people of Jesus' day reacted to Him, and the message He brought to them, we need to understand about how He used the meal table.

One writer said that in Luke's Gospel, 'Jesus is either going to a meal, at a meal, or coming from a meal'.[4] This is

---

[4] R J Karris, *Eating Your Way through Luke's Gospel* (Collegeville: Liturgical Press, 2006), p 14.

a bit of a deliberate exaggeration, but makes the point. Jesus eats with all kinds of people, but especially those who are excluded in some way. Tax collectors such as Levi and Zacchaeus – hated and considered traitors by their own people. Prostitutes, who Jesus said were coming into the kingdom ahead of the religious leaders (see Matthew 21:31). He ate with the 'sinners' – probably a known group rather than just anyone who had sinned, perhaps including prostitutes and others who, through their jobs, clearly were continuing to sin. He eats with women, and possibly Gentiles – the feeding of the 4,000 was in Gentile territory.

As well as this list of undesirables, Jesus also eats with Pharisees and teachers of the law – those respected in society. So it is a varied list of companions. Sometimes Jesus is the host, as in the feeding of the 4,000 and 5,000, and the Last Supper, but more often He is a guest. As an invited guest, He had the right to bring others with Him, so He would often be the annoying guest who turned up at well-to-do parties with His unlikely crew of sinners, peasants and outcasts!

Jesus does all this as what we might call an 'acted parable'. As well as all the parables He told and the teaching He gave, His very choice of table companions was a powerful message in itself. What, then, was He saying through these acted parables?

In true preacher's style, I have five points all starting with H. I am not proud of this as I try to avoid such cheesiness if at all possible. But it might help you to remember them.

Hierarchy

At Jesus' table, hierarchy is abolished. Jesus subverts the idea that some people are more important than others owing to their background or their role in society. Imagine Jesus as host, getting the children and the sinners to sit next to Him in the places of honour. He even tells His disciples in Luke 14:10 to seek out the lowest places at the meals. This is the opposite of what they would have been taught by their parents growing up! But in the kingdom of Jesus, the path to honour comes through humility. The way to become great is to become the least. The first will be last, and the last, first. In a world where people are promoting their 'brand' on social media, trying to go viral and have their ten minutes of fame, this is an important challenge.

This idea would have been shocking to Jews and pagans alike. Who does this man think He is? Children were of little worth in his day, quite the opposite to today, but He valued them and honoured them. Women were also distrusted – their testimonies were not valid in a court of law, and yet Jesus even allowed Mary to sit at His feet in Luke 10:39 – a description of a rabbi training a disciple so that she could eventually become a rabbi herself. This happened in a house, and therefore would almost certainly have involved food.

At Jesus' table, all were of equal value – slaves, women, tax collectors, sinners, prostitutes, religious leaders – even Gentiles. I wonder if this is why He asked us to remember Him not by saying a certain prayer or by reading a particular story, but by eating a meal? Eating is one thing that all humans have to do, and it can remind us that we are all the same; especially when we break bread and pass around a cup of wine, remembering that we have all sinned and need to have our hunger and thirst satisfied by Jesus.

Holiness

The people of God knew they were called to be a holy, set-apart people. Moses had given them the command from the mouth of God: 'Be holy to me because I, the Lord, am holy' (Leviticus 20:26). This involved keeping to the laws of God designed to make them different to the nations around them because 'I have set you apart from the nations to be my own'.

For the Pharisees and Essenes, holiness was something to be fenced off and protected. They did this by drawing clear lines between what was clean and unclean. They would demonstrate who was clean and who was unclean – who was in and who was out – by who was allowed at the table. If they came into contact with anyone or anything unclean, their holiness was polluted and defiled.

At Jesus' table, this attitude to holiness is reversed. Jesus actively finds those who are unclean, and touches them. He describes Himself as a doctor (Mark 2:17), and doctors need to touch their patients in order to bring healing. Jesus touches the leper, the woman with the problem with bleeding, and a dead girl, among many others. All three of these actions would have made Him ceremonially unclean. But something new is happening in Jesus' kingdom, and at Jesus' table.

Jesus' touch has the opposite effect. Instead of Him being polluted and His holiness made unholy, the process reverses and Jesus' holiness flows into the person – making the leper clean, stopping the woman's bleeding, and raising the dead girl to life. A new thing is happening in this kingdom of the new creation. The touch, the welcome to the table comes first. No longer do you need to get clean before you come to the table of God. The welcome to all happens first.

But then comes the transformation. It comes not by our own efforts, but from meeting with Jesus Himself. A couple of years ago I was speaking at a youth meeting and told them that Jesus invites them to come to Him right now, just as they are, without getting everything sorted out and making themselves clean first. Afterwards a girl came to me and said, 'You know that stuff you said about coming to Jesus just as you are and not needing to clean up first? Is that actually true?' I was slightly offended at the idea I might say something untrue! She said, 'I always felt like I was too much of a bad person to be a Christian. Does that mean I can become a Christian now?' You certainly can!

A few weeks ago she emailed me to say that her life has been totally transformed since that day. She is now doing a gap year serving in her local church and finding meaning and freedom in her life. What happened to her was what happened at Jesus' table then and now. A welcome, then a transformation.

We have seen this many times. Our job is to provide the welcome in Jesus' name, then Jesus brings the transformation. Recently we invited children from the local school to come to church and perform a play, and to bring their parents. The kids were excited, the parents not quite so happy at being taken out of their usual Sunday routines!

A couple of the parents made it quite clear to us that as soon as the play finished, they would be leaving. They sat at the tables with their arms folded, making their displeasure known.

Then the change began. As our church people welcomed them and ate with them, they softened. As their children performed a sketch of the David and Goliath story, they relaxed and began to smile. When I started to give my talk they all stayed to listen, and as I spoke about how God can give us courage to overcome the giants in our own lives, they nodded in agreement. The two who had said they were rushing off ended up staying the longest and going up to our prayer room to look around! At Jesus' table, transformation happens.

An older guy from the estate started coming along to church. As I led communion one Sunday, he came to receive it for the first time. He told me that he had never felt he could take communion because of what he had done in the past, but when I said that day that Jesus welcomes everyone to His table, he realised that he was included too. He came with the rest of the church, and Jesus welcomed him with open arms. This led to a number of experiences of God for him, where he realised how much God loved him and that He forgave him for the past. This has happened with a number of people. They have always felt excluded or unclean, then they are invited to Jesus' table, and feel a sense of belonging for the first time. Jesus welcomes us, then changes us.

Change happens at Jesus' table. And it can be costly – think about Zacchaeus! A meal with Jesus can utterly transform our lives, and the lives of those around us.

Healing is given

In the Gospels, it appears that healing and hospitality are like two sides of the same coin. When Jesus sends out the seventy-two in Luke 10, Jesus commands them to take nothing with them, but rely on the hospitality of those they are sent to reach. As the people in the village receive them and feed them, the disciples are instructed to heal all the sick people. Hospitality and healing belong together. Levi and Zacchaeus are both transformed when they receive Jesus into their homes for food, and this link between hospitality and healing can also be found in the Old Testament – for example, in the story of Elisha and the rich woman in 2 Kings 4, or Abraham's welcome to the three strangers in Genesis 18.

Hospitality and healing, meals and miracles. As we have eaten together over the years as a church, we have seen this connection – both in dramatic, sudden moments when people experience God in a life-changing way, and in slow, steady changes as people gradually discover that they are welcomed and loved for who they are, and slowly open up like a flower on a sunny day. Both are beautiful to see, and both are given by God.

Hunger is key

As I call people to come and take communion, I increasingly find myself saying, 'If you're hungry for Jesus, come and receive from Him now.' At Jesus' table, hunger gives you access, rather than holiness or hierarchy. I believe there is a deep hunger for spiritual reality in the world today. We see this in the response of people being offered healing prayer. We have seen it as, year after year, we have taken members of our church football team, with no previous experience of church, to the Soul Survivor festivals. Every time, the parts they enjoy most are the times of prayer ministry, when people respond to God in interesting ways! They nearly all end up asking for prayer, and encountering the Holy Spirit in some way.

I have also noticed this hunger among our local children. When we take communion in church, the children are the first to come up to receive. For the last two years we have set up a prayer room in the local community primary school, and it has been overwhelmed with children wanting to come and pray. It was hunger that led Matty to his experience of interpreting tongues. Jesus always responds to our hunger for Him. Jesus described Himself as the Bread of Life and on the last day of the Feast of Tabernacles, stood up and said, 'Let anyone who is thirsty come to me and drink' (John 7:37, NIV 2011).

Hope is given

We have already looked at how the Church is supposed to be a glimpse of God's future for the world – this is particularly true when it comes to Jesus' table. It has an *eschatological* aspect to it; demonstrating what the coming kingdom of God will look like. It is a taster of things to come, of the great Messianic banquet prophesied by Isaiah: 'On this mountain the LORD Almighty will prepare a feast of rich food for all peoples, a banquet of aged wine – the best of meats and the finest of wines' (Isaiah 25:6).

Isaiah saw that the feast would include all peoples, including the Gentiles, and Jesus then demonstrated that it would also include all the most unlikely people in every walk of life. The poor, the marginalised and the sinners. Jesus told the Pharisees that the tax collectors and prostitutes were coming into the kingdom ahead of them (see Matthew 21:31). This use of the table as an eschatological window into the coming kingdom was possibly the most offensive and controversial aspect of Jesus' table fellowship.

It is an interesting task to think, 'If Jesus was here in my country today, who would He have around His table?' Immigrants, asylum seekers, refugees – He would be valuing them and showing them true hospitality, as well as accepting their hospitality. But it is a harder task to imagine Him eating with those of whom I would disapprove.

For me as a Manchester United fan, that might mean Liverpool and Man City fans (*shudders*)! Or perhaps members of a far-right group, spewing their hatred to all who would listen? Jesus, don't eat with them, it would ruin Your reputation! There would be pictures going viral all over social media. Or what about a known terrorist sympathiser?

This is what happened to Jesus. By associating with the people most hated in society, He actually became associated with them in people's minds, and was accused of being 'a glutton and a drunkard, a friend of tax collectors and "sinners"' (Matthew 11:19). And the second part of the allegation was entirely true.

My parents came to visit one weekend, and came to church on Sunday. As they walked towards the entrance, our welcoming committee was there to greet them. On this day there was a haze of cigarette smoke to get through, and some colourful language being used. Afterwards my dad had a quiet word with me. 'Son, I think it's great how you're reaching all these people with the gospel. But when I arrived through the smoke and swearing – should this be people's first impression of Langworthy Community Church? Do you think that group should be representing you, forming people's first impressions of you?'

I thought long and hard about this, as I respect my parents more than anyone else in the world. They have modelled to me how to live the Christian life. But I had to disagree with some of what my dad said. When it comes down to it, I do want people to see those guys on the door as representing LCC. Not giving the whole picture, of course, but I want people to look and say, 'I could belong there. Whoever I am, I could find a home there.' I want our church to be so associated with the poor, the disadvantaged and the sinners, that people might be tempted to accuse us as they did Jesus.

I will never forget our first-ever church weekend away when we invited some families from our estate who hadn't been to church before. One family brought so much alcohol that their room was effectively a small off-licence! They were very generous with their stash, which was kind but not too helpful when we had three recovering alcoholics in the church at the time. I dread to think what the people at the Christian conference centre thought of us. That was a lesson quickly learned.

Jesus' example of living His life with those on the edges of society is a huge challenge to us not only as churches, but as individuals too. One writer makes a distinction between acts of charity, and what he calls 'commensality'. Strictly speaking, commensality is to bond together with someone over food and drink, but this scholar uses it to refer to a lifestyle rather than just a one-off meal.

It would have been common in Jesus' day to put on meals for poor people as acts of charity, just as many churches do at Christmas today for homeless people. This is not what Jesus is doing. He is including all these marginalised people not just at the occasional meal, but in His life, at His own table.

One example could be useful here. I give £20 a month to sponsor a child called Yolanda in Zimbabwe. This is a good and important thing to do. But it isn't difficult. I hardly notice the money leaving my account each month, and it eases my conscience to know I am helping someone worse off than me. But Yolanda makes almost no impact on my life. This is the kind of charity which is useful, but not what Jesus did. The writer I referred to earlier says that this kind of charity is 'our last desperate defence against the terror of commensality'.[5]

When all our connections with those different to us are based on the modern idea of charity, we are able to hold people at arm's length, while easing our consciences that we are making a difference in the world. Jesus goes much further than this, and challenges us to do the same. Your church may run a food bank, but who sits around your dinner table? Whom do I invite to my parties? Have I ever taken Jesus' words seriously when He said, 'When you give a luncheon or dinner, do not invite your friends, your

[5] J D Crossan, *The Historical Jesus* (New York: HarperOne, 1991), p 341.

brothers or relatives … invite the poor, the crippled, the lame, the blind, and you will be blessed' (Luke 14:12-14). As always, this is not just something Jesus said, but something He lived out.

It is a difficult challenge for all of us. A year after Esther and I were married, I was mentoring a local lad called Andy (not his real name). Andy became a Christian, and was really keen in his new-found faith. He was from a difficult background. He hadn't seen his dad since he was young, when his dad told him he was going to the shop, and never bothered to return. His relationship with his mother was more like a friendship than a parent and child.

When his mum had to move away when he was seventeen, Esther and I decided to have him live with us. We had these romantic ideas about being able to show him what a loving family could be like, to have two people who loved him for who he was. It was great for six months, and then things started to fall apart.

We noticed he had been smoking in his room, and asked him to stop. Then the smell of smoke became sweeter, and smelt more… illegal. We found mysterious powder lying around. Then money started to go missing, more money than we could afford to lose. I refused to believe it was him, but eventually we established that he was definitely stealing. The situation reached a level where it was no longer safe for him to live with us, and he moved out.

We were both devastated. We loved him, and he had taken a piece of us with him as he left (as well as my iPod and several other items). There is no happy ending to this story. The last time I heard from Andy he was spending his nights at work and his days smoking weed and playing computer games.

When I occasionally tell Andy's story as I am preaching, I point out that it is one of the worst preacher's stories ever. People expect it to end with 'and now he has come back to God and is travelling the country leading hundreds of people to Jesus! And he went back to school and aced his A levels.' But it doesn't. And that is something that happens when we follow Jesus into a life of commensality with those who are different, or 'other', to us.

Of course, that kind of thing would never have happened to Jesus, would it? Investing your life in someone for months or even years, only for them to throw it back in your face? Well, there was Judas. And all the others who abandoned Him when He needed them the most. Judas can seem obvious to us in hindsight, but he must have been out with the other disciples, casting out demons and healing the sick, otherwise the others would have been suspicious ('Why is Judas always staying in and just counting the money?'). Jesus would have invested so much love and time into Judas, sharing His life with him just as with the other eleven – watching him try and fail, try and succeed, laying on hands and seeing people healed for the first time. Think of all those shared memories over three long years, surviving as a group through persecution, seeing extraordinary miraculous events, experiencing love in its purest form. And yet still Judas betrayed Jesus. I wonder whether the more we follow the example and teaching of Jesus, the more of these kind of stories we should expect. It isn't an easy path, but Jesus will be there with us in it.

Church at its best is a ragtag collection of misfits, feasting together around a table next to a roaring fire, people you would never expect to find all together in one room, except for a miracle. As the earliest Christians took the good news of Jesus around the world, they took the huge step of sharing their tables with Gentiles. This was one of the main causes of conflict with their Jewish roots, and would eventually contribute to Christianity becoming not just a Jewish Messianic sect, but a religion in its own right.

It is clear from the New Testament that the earliest Church continued to hold their worship gatherings around meal tables, providing hospitality and a welcome to marginalised people, and as they ate together, they would break bread and share wine as Jesus had taught them to do. They would meet the risen Jesus at their tables – as the two disciples did on the road to Emmaus; as they did over a barbecue on the beach in John 21; when He promised them the Holy Spirit in Acts 1:4. In Revelation 3:20, Jesus promises to meet with his people as they eat: 'If you hear my voice and open the door, I will come in to you and eat with you, and you with me' (NRSV).

Eating a meal was so important for the early Church that the earliest description we have of Christians from a non-Christian, Pliny the Younger (early second century), identifies the distinctive practices of the Christians as worshipping Jesus as a god, living holy lives, and eating a regular meal together. Pliny was writing from modern-day Turkey, showing that the meal remained important as the Church spread around the world.

As the years and decades passed, the Christian communal meal (sometimes called 'the *agape'* or love-feast) became separate from the ritual of breaking bread and drinking wine, until eventually it died out altogether. The ritual meal took on characteristics of other meals in Jewish and pagan society, helping the Christians to define who was in and who was out – only the baptised could come to the Lord's table. Instead of the welcome coming first, a degree of holiness was again required to gain access to the table.

This is not the place to make an argument about the rights and wrongs of restricting access to communion, or Eucharist. But it does seem as though the Church lost something very precious from those earliest days – this joyful, controversially inclusive and central meal begun by Jesus and carried on by the earliest Church – and it would be wonderful if we can try to recapture some of this in our day and age, where loneliness is so rampant.

This study of Jesus' meals often encourages me as I look around our church on a Sunday and see this eclectic, chaotic group of people, all on a messy journey of faith together, all hungry for Jesus and praying to meet Him as we eat together.

This is how Acts describes the meals of the earliest Church, and what happened at them:

> They devoted themselves to the apostles' teaching and to the fellowship, to the breaking of bread and to prayer. Everyone was filled with awe, and many wonders and miraculous signs were done by the apostles. All the believers were together and had everything in common. Selling

their possessions and goods, they gave to anyone as he had need. Every day they continued to meet together in the temple courts. They broke bread in their homes and ate together with glad and sincere hearts, praising God and enjoying the favour of all the people. And the Lord added to their number daily those who were being saved.
Acts 2:42-47

Deep community, teaching, prayer, miracles, generosity, sacrificial living, joy, worship, daily salvation. Let us pray for more tables like that one!

Chapter 5
The Gift of Stability

I will never forget hearing Andy Hawthorne first explain the vision for the Eden project. '80 per cent of Christians live in the suburbs, where 20 per cent of the people live. Only 20 per cent of Christians live in the inner cities, where 80 per cent of the people live. This has got to change!' I found myself nodding my head in agreement. I had already sensed a call to move into Langworthy. Andy continued, 'But we're not just talking about a gap year here, or a project for a couple of years. We're calling you to commit to a minimum of *five* years!' Wow. Five years seemed like an awfully long time to a guy in his early twenties. What if I didn't like it? I couldn't imagine what I'd be doing in one year, let alone five.

As that call rang out on various big stages at Christian festivals, many other young adults responded to the call. A call to serious commitment. A call to sacrifice your ambitions, to put aside a desire for a comfortable life in a nice area for the sake of the gospel. I was part of the interview process for a number of earnest eighteen to twenty-somethings, all passionate about serving Jesus, all keen to move into the neighbourhood and see the streams flowing in the desert. I would always pray that God would give them the character to persevere when times got tough.

Five years. Looking back now, eighteen years on, five years is a tiny amount of time. It seemed such a huge commitment to make, such a sacrifice for the Lord! But the reality is that in the inner city, after five years you are only just beginning to scratch the surface of all that could be done. After ten, you are starting to see some fruit.

This long-term outlook was not in any way in my mind as I moved into Langworthy. The mid to late 1990s was a time of huge expectation in the Christian circles I was in. Prophecies of revival were everywhere – it was a matter of when, rather than if, revival was coming to the UK, and where would it start? I hoped and half-expected it to be in Langworthy.

My closest friends and I had a real expectation that revival was coming to Salford, and that it probably would be a matter of weeks or months from us moving in until we saw it hit Langworthy. What it would look like was unclear; we assumed it would involve hundreds of young people coming to faith, and their families (you and your whole household … see Acts 16:31) encountering Jesus too, and healings and miracles all over the place.

We threw ourselves into a full programme of outreach, with no real planning for a sustainable lifestyle for the long term, just putting everything into it in order to see this revival come. People were burning out but we kept going. Visiting speakers encouraged us to press on. 'Don't call in sick – crawl in sick! Spend yourselves on behalf of the hungry!' So we did. And as a result, many people only lasted a matter of months, or a year or two, before moving on, tired and disillusioned.

When we launched the LifeCentre in 2000, we were not only told that it would be burned down in six months, but one or two locals made a more telling prediction. 'You'll only last for two or three years, like all the projects that come here.' This is the experience of countless inner-city communities across the country. Some funding is obtained for a project, it makes a big splash for a year or two, then the funding runs out and all the relationships and networks are lost.

It happens with churches too. On a couple of occasions during our time in Langworthy, a church has hired a local building, run outreach programmes and built local relationships, then left after two or three years when their cars were consistently broken into, or a building in a nicer area became available. And then the Church as a whole is tarred with the same brush. 'You're only here when it suits you.' This is surely the opposite of the reputation we want the Church to have.

The Church at its best can give a wonderful gift to the community where it is based: the gift of stability. This is something I have admired about my friends in the Anglican Church – that vision of having a church for every part of the country. When a friend of mine planted a church in another estate, the local Anglican vicar said to him, 'We were here a long time before you came, and we will be here a long time after you leave.' The vicar was rude, but he was right. That church plant quickly moved elsewhere, but the estate still has a church there whose job it is to pray for them and serve them.

Of course, it's all very well having a church building with a vicar who is in theory committed to serving the community, but in order to see real change, the whole church congregation has to get hold of the idea of stability, and prayerfully consider giving this gift to the community. Stability works itself out and has the greatest effect in genuine relationships, rather than just geographical proximity and 'being available', as important as these things are. You could live in a community for your whole life, but have very little impact. It all depends on how you love people and choose to serve, and listen.

To illustrate this let me tell you about Kane. Kane grew up in Langworthy, living with his mum and sister. Life at home was often difficult, and Kane describes it as 'dysfunctional with a spectrum of issues'. We first came into contact with him as an eight-year-old when one of our team, Liz, found him sitting on the wall of her backyard, throwing stones. Liz, being one of the most godly and incredible people you will ever meet, decided not to push him off the wall but to get to know him, and soon she was giving him piano lessons and getting to know his family. Kane gradually found belonging, family and, above all, acceptance.

Years later, we baptised Kane in a freezing cold children's paddling pool amid much shrieking because of the cold, and an awkward moment when we realised there wasn't enough water to immerse him fully, so we used a bucket to finish the job! Kane's testimony that day was a revelation to me: 'I first met youse lot when I was sitting on Liz's wall throwing stones. Then I met Greg and Andrew, who had moved into the next street. Then I met Sarah, Natalie [the list goes on]. Then we moved away so I didn't see anyone for a while.' (Note: He only moved to another part of Salford.)

'Then we moved back into Langworthy and Sandra told me there was a new church she was going to, and they had food and free trips out. So I went along and found that the trips weren't free. But Liz, Natalie, Andrew, Greg and everyone were still there, and I got to know Chris, Esther, Rachel and others. I liked everyone at church so started going along. Then I went to Soul Survivor and became a Christian.'

I loved Kane's story that day because it was about three things: stability, community and proximity. Kane met Liz and the rest of the team because of *proximity*, and that is the reason he made those friendships that endured. He lived on Liz's street, so he saw her most days and she became a part of his life. When his family moved back to Langworthy, most of those people he had known before were still there, and at church he received the gift of *stability*. A group of people who would be there not for a few months, but for many years. And he discovered in that phase of his life a new *community*, where he would not be judged, but loved and invested in. While he went through years of wrestling with his identity, and having issues with addiction and mental health, in the church he discovered the love, grace and mercy of God. He told me, 'Had LCC people not taught me and shown me love and acceptance, I can say with confidence that my life would not be different, but non-existent. I have faced suicidal thoughts a few times in the last eight years … God is the reason I am alive … that doesn't mean everything is great all the time, but it does mean God is with me all the time.'

Often stories like Kane's end there, in the land of Happy Ever After. Real life is different. I could end it there, or I could end it when I dropped him off at Bible college to start his theology degree. Or I could end the story a year later when he dropped out of Bible college feeling that he couldn't carry on, crushed by depression. But it didn't end there either. He had the bravery to go back the next year, and is now in his final year, battling to get it done. He wants to go on into ministry in the Church, reaching the marginalised and broken with the hope and love he has experienced.

The truth is, Kane's story is not finished. He will have more ups and downs. I pray that he will have more ups than downs, and that God will continue to bring healing to him so he would know life in all its fullness. One thing Kane knows, though, is that I'm still here whenever he may need me. Our team are still present in Langworthy, working away as we always have done, trying to love people as Jesus does. That is a great gift that we can give. I hope we can play a part in the next chapter of Kane's story, but wherever he ends up, he knows where to find us.

Another important point is that if we had all fulfilled our radical five-year commitment and then moved on, having done our time in the inner city, we would never have had the honour of baptising Kane and being alongside him through all the huge lows and wonderful highs of his teenage years.

If we had only done two Eden shifts – a full ten years – we would never have had the privilege of working with children and young people, as we do today, whose parents were in our youth programmes in those early years of our work in Langworthy. This is a wonderful benefit of stability, because the parents now know us and trust us. They are confident that the church is for them, and that we want the best for their family and for the whole estate.

I am convinced that when we reach a third generation in our estate, we will enter a new phase of breakthrough in our mission. The Bible refers to the effect of sin on families 'to the third and fourth generation' (for example, Exodus 20:5), and I believe this can also apply with blessing and goodness. In ancient Israel, three or four generations would live in close proximity to each other, thus having a huge influence on each other's lives. This is also the case in such estates as Langworthy, where extended families often live on the same street. One life transformed by God can have a huge effect on many others.

In our work, we have seen two quite different responses to God's work in people's lives. Some people respond quickly, and change rapidly, often in a quite dramatic fashion. Others are slow burners, who can be around a long time until you suddenly notice that a wonderful miracle has happened. Both these responses require the gift of stability in order to help the individual flourish. I will now give you an example of each, and what we have learned from their lives.

We met Gemma in the early days of the Eden Salford project. She was loud, hilarious and very likeable. She would also get into trouble a lot at school. She started to attend some of the Eden lunch clubs in her school, and once a month we would invite all the young people with whom we were in touch to the Planet Life event at Manchester Apollo. Planet Life was a huge, loud, dynamic outreach event involving famous Christians giving their testimonies, performances from well-known Christian bands (always including the legends that were the World Wide Message Tribe!) and evangelists preaching for a response. It was like a Christian variety show, but cool.

Gemma came along on the coach one Sunday night with some of her mates, making sure she'd had plenty of alcohol first so she was quite drunk when she arrived. At the end of the night, when there was a call for young people to give their lives to Jesus, Gemma found herself processing out with many others into a side room, where the young people were spoken to about the commitment they had just made, and given some literature to help them on their new journey with Jesus.

Just a drunk teenager, in a highly charged emotional setting, being taken along with the crowd. What good could come of that? Gemma felt different after that day. She had fallen out with her dad and hadn't spoken to him for two years. She went and made peace with him. Her teachers were stunned when she came into school and apologised to them all for her bad behaviour in school, and were just as surprised when she started working hard and managed to get a great set of grades in her GCSEs and A levels!

Because of her excellent communication skills, Gemma quickly became a bit of a 'poster girl' in Greater Manchester, finding herself on lots of different stages telling her story of salvation. The local churches loved hearing this incredible story of transformation – this surely was what Eden was all about? The more middle-class audiences always applauded when she shared about getting great exam results!

This was a real and wonderful transformation. But there is much more to Gemma's story. After a couple of years of telling the story above, I remember talking to her and saying how great that story was, but what about more recent stories? What has God done recently for you? Gemma shared with me that her faith had begun to feel like a set of rules that were really difficult to stick to, rather than the dynamic story of her first encounters with God. I felt that she was trapped in a world of being one person on stage, and the reality of her life in the day to day. She had been put on a pedestal. She wasn't losing her faith, but she was having struggles with living the Christian life, and it was difficult to continue telling a 'happily ever after' story when real life was quite different.

What does stability have to do with Gemma's story? The friends Gemma had made were not going anywhere. We would always be here for her. Whether she came regularly to church or not, we were still her friends who loved her and wanted the best for her life. While she went through various crises in her walk with God, we could walk with her. Stability is not just about continuing to live in a certain area, it is about a commitment to loving people in the long term, not dependent on how they respond to your efforts to evangelise or disciple them.

Another friend of ours is Susan. She is much quieter and more understated than Gemma, and was part of that same generation of young people who first came to the Planet Life events. Susan didn't respond to the calls to go into the room and become a Christian. When we spoke to her about it, she said, 'I like you lot 'cos you're really nice people.' (She was right. We were, and are, *really* nice.) 'But I'm a good person too,' she continued. 'And so I don't think I really need to become a Christian.'

Sometimes people would see our church and notice how we had many people who came regularly but didn't identify as Christian. I would be asked, 'It's all great having people coming along to church like this. But what if they don't become Christians after, like, five years?' I would say, 'What do you think we should do? Kick them out? Smack them with a Bible? Let them come along but they have to sit on their own table in the corner? The non-Christian table?' The answer, of course, is that we love them! Susan was part of us for seven years before she made a decision to follow Jesus. Occasionally she would say, 'I might become a Christian next year' just to tease us. When she eventually took the plunge, I asked her how things had changed. She said, 'It's like going from black and white TV to colour TV.' Brilliant.

The gift of stability meant that Susan could come to Jesus in her own time without being rushed, or judged, or excluded. The gift of stability meant that Gemma, when doubts and difficulties came, could process them in the context of a loving community who would still love and accept her, even if she had decided to reject the faith entirely. There is a huge danger when someone like Gemma, who is also a great communicator, becomes a Christian in a dramatic way that we elevate them into a celebrity, parading them like a trophy representing our missional success. When we elevate someone in such a way, we are just giving them further to fall. It was fortunate for Gemma that she had that gift of stability given to her by her Christian friends.

What is Gemma up to now, you may ask? She is living with her husband in Tenerife, having just passed her MA with distinction (cue the applause), and hilariously – given her experiences through most of school – she is now a teacher! She also continues her journey with God. She comes to us for prayer and advice (at one point I was known as her Facebook Pastor!) but is now able to find her own stability, and to offer that to the children she is teaching.

This is the effect of the gift of stability, that we can give to others. Gemma's story, and that of Brian, whom you met in the introduction, are dramatic. 'I used to do this … then I had this experience of God … now I'm like this – totally different.' Evangelical Christians love these stories, they are the stories that encourage us that this thing really works. We would prefer the stories not to have the difficult bits afterwards, of course, but generally Gemma's conversion story is preferred to Susan's, because of the drama involved. Also, it's easier to take someone to a big event and in one moment, everything changes, rather than spending hours and days and months and years investing in someone, and seeing gradual changes that sometimes don't even last.

My friend who for me, exemplifies the effect of stability, is called Turkey. Obviously he isn't really called Turkey, but it's one of those nicknames that has stuck so much that if I call him James, it feels weird. We met Turkey when he was about ten and he used to mess around in our youth activities. He was quite a regular throughout his teens, but

I always felt he was mainly there for a laugh and for the girls, rather than with any interest in God. I felt as if he didn't really get the whole God thing. I also was concerned that, being a natural people-person and peer leader, he would be leading the more committed ones astray. I was right.

Turkey got into all the usual teenage stuff in Salford – drink, drugs, girls. He had difficulties at home too. But he kept coming to youth activities, including small groups looking at the Bible, and to church on Sundays. With his peer group he would spend hours at the houses of some of our church people – Greg and Abbie, who opened their home to so many over many years, and later, Martin and Yvonne, an incredible couple a decade (or maybe a few) older than most of us, who courageously obeyed God's call to join us to be grandparents to our young church.

One year I remember taking some young lads to Soul Survivor and a couple of them asking to become Christians. That particular year we decided to encourage the lads to wait till they got home, then make a decision away from the emotion of it all. My brother (Ar Kid) remembers the day after we got home, getting a call from one of the lads to say, 'Andy, can I become a Christian yet?' Then, in the next two days, the same thing happened a couple more times with different lads! Andrew wondered whether that was revival – you just sit at home and people call you to ask if they're allowed to become Christians!

Turkey came to me around that time and said, 'Can I do a Bible study for the lads, you know, like teaching them about how to be Christians?' I was really surprised but said, 'Err… yes, that sounds great!' So he started that with some help from others. A while later, he said, 'Can I open the LifeCentre once a week for the local young people to come in, and so they have somewhere to hang out and we can tell them about God?' Well, yes, that would be great! So he gathered a team and opened it up.

At the time of writing, Turkey is the main youth worker in our church. He is married to Lucy, another amazing Salford legend, and is devoting his life to helping others and bringing children and young people to know Jesus. It's not just a flash in the pan but a consistent growth that is blessing others. He's just a brilliant lad. Sometimes I look back and I think, how did that happen? *When* did it happen? When was that moment when he got on his knees before God and left his past behind and everything changed? And the truth is, there wasn't a moment. Or more accurately, there were hundreds of moments. Moments when Greg and Abbie didn't feel like having him and his mates round, but chose to anyway. Moments when we believed in him enough to let him lead that youth drop-in. Moments when Martin and Yvonne saw past his behaviour into his heart, and called out his potential. The countless hours when he received the gift of stability into a life that had often been unstable.

This story is a miracle. It's as much of a miracle as the healings we've seen, or Brian's deliverance from addiction, or Gemma's turnaround. But it isn't spectacular, and it takes longer to tell it. You could call it an *ordinary miracle.* And they are the kind of miracles we have seen most during the eighteen years we have been doing this stuff. Ordinary miracles. If you blink you might miss them. Keep your eyes open, and you see them everywhere. God is always at work, advancing His kingdom, and we need to see and recognise it, to tell the stories, to call out the potential, to love people unconditionally for the long term. Susan's story is an ordinary miracle. So is mine.

Another aspect of stability is being stable in who we are as a church – you could call it being trustworthy. This is what we have seen in our relationships with the other community groups. When I first spoke to the local church leaders about planting a new church, there was a natural unease. Would we steal their people? I assured them we wouldn't, but that was only words. When it became obvious that we were actively discouraging local Christians from joining us, people started to trust us more. One man on a local church PCC used to call us 'the enemy', but his fears were unfounded as the years went by.

We got involved with the local schools, becoming governors, helping with behavioural problems, providing mentoring, and generally serving however we could, not on our terms but the schools' terms. We were able to prove over many years that we could be trusted – we were not just some crazy Bible-bashers wanting to get involved in order to impose our agenda and sneak in a Christian message, but simply to work for the common good. As Jeremiah 29:7 says, 'Seek the peace and prosperity of the city … Pray to the LORD for it, because if it prospers, you too will prosper.'

We are quite clear about our faith – it is Jesus who motivates us to serve in all these ways – but we will not take advantage of the trust that is given to us. We will be worthy of the trust given. Sometimes we have had Christian groups standing in front of schoolchildren with the idea that this could be the only time these kids will hear 'the gospel', so they want to give it to them, launching into all sorts of inappropriate descriptions of hell and trying to threaten people into the kingdom. The gift of stability means that we are not in a rush. We wait for God to lead us. We don't have to have a manic approach that doesn't value the work of others. Relationships that have been built up over many years in an estate can be damaged hugely by an over-enthusiastic preacher with a Messiah complex.

We now run weeks in the local schools where all the children get to visit a prayer room, and have the experience of encountering the presence of God. We have been asked, by school leaders who are not Christians, to run groups in school time where the children can learn more about Christianity and explore their faith. This is because of the gift of stability. If we were unable to do such things, we would still serve the schools. But the friendships lead to trust, a trust we must be worthy of, and we work hard to continue to earn that trust. One of the things the staff appreciate about our team is that they live in the area, so will see the children outside school hours and can continue to build on the positive influence that begins in the classroom.

In our hyper-mobile world, God is calling some people to a countercultural life of stability. To invest in one place for the next decade and beyond. To be a people who are not in a rush, but live in God's time. To not always be thinking of where next, but to embed ourselves in a community, to feel the heartbeat of that place, to sow the seeds of the gospel there and see what grows up. When you plant a tree, it will often be enjoyed most by people beyond your lifetime. When we plant ourselves in a community, we need to invest in such a way as to see long-term growth and transformation, rather than fighting for quick results that make us look good but ultimately burn us out and then we move on. Let's seek the well-being of the places God has called us to, and pray to the Lord for them.

I would like to push this a little further and suggest that where we choose to live and how long we choose to stay there is one of the key discipleship issues of our time. Often young leaders feel 'called' to the bright lights and the big churches. I would dearly love it if this chapter might influence some of you to rethink your ambitions. Perhaps there is a talented musician reading this whose ambition it is to become a worship pastor in a successful church. Maybe you might take a different path, and move into a forgotten community and get to know the local young people. Give them music lessons, help them form a band. Show them how to meet Jesus in their music. More importantly, don't leave when it gets tough. Walk with them through their teenage years and love them for who they are. The way of Jesus is not one of prominence, but servanthood.

Chapter 6
Don't Give Up

It had been a difficult year. A close friend of ours had died suddenly, and around the same time, Esther had a miscarriage. There were some difficult pastoral issues going on in the church. I had noticed I was getting regular migraines and tension headaches. We had a fortnight's holiday coming up, so I asked my trustees if I could have two extra weeks off and turn it into a month-long sabbatical. They agreed and I decided this could be just what I needed to get me back on track.

About halfway through the month off, I began to realise what a state I was in. Physically I felt even worse than when I had begun the sabbatical. Headaches, dizziness and tiredness were the daily norm. I felt fearful about my future, about my health, and I could barely think straight. I told Esther that I couldn't possibly imagine how I could get to a stage where I would feel ready to return to work. Even the thought of it made me feel afraid and deeply inadequate. I called it my 'year of fear'.

Six or more years on from that point, I look back and think of what carried me through that time. I did manage to return to work, stronger and wiser than before, and have avoided that kind of crash ever since. If we are to give people the gift of stability described in the last chapter, part of what is needed is wisdom in how to keep going in the difficult times. For me this came from a number of sources: Scripture, friends, prophetic encouragement and the power of hope. This is by no means an exclusive list, but this is what helped me and I hope might be helpful to others. All of these things can be useful whatever your calling in life, but especially when your calling involves working in particularly difficult circumstances or places.

Scripture

Paul writes to the church in Rome:

> Therefore, since we have been justified through faith, we have peace with God through our Lord Jesus Christ, through whom we have gained access by faith into this grace in which we now stand. And we rejoice in the hope of the glory of God. Not only so, but we also rejoice in our sufferings, because we know that suffering produces perseverance; perseverance, character; and character, hope. And hope does not disappoint us, because God has poured out his love into our hearts by the Holy Spirit, whom he has given us.
> *Romans 5:1-5*

In this challenging passage, Paul rejoices in two things. The first is *the hope of the glory of God.* In the darkest times, there is always hope. There is the ultimate Christian hope that one day God will put the world to rights once and for all – the knowledge of the glory of the Lord will cover the earth as the waters cover the sea, as Habakkuk put it (2:14).

And that future hope gives us hope too, as we pray the prayer that Jesus taught us: 'your kingdom come, your will be done on earth as it is in heaven' (Matthew 6:10). We can see glimpses of that future glory in our lives now, just like those spies who ate the grapes of the Promised Land while they were still in the desert.

We can nod in agreement, then, when Paul talks about rejoicing in the hope of the glory of God. This can encourage us, as it did for me, that there is a light at the end of every tunnel. However, now things get rather strange – 'we also rejoice in our sufferings'. What? Is Paul some kind of masochist, who welcomes, or even seeks out, suffering? Is he like some of the desert ascetics of the early Christian centuries who used to tie themselves to tall poles and allow maggots to live in their wounds, thinking that somehow they were becoming closer to Jesus as a result?

What Paul is actually doing here is sketching out a path from suffering to hope. A hope that does not disappoint us. Paul is not rejoicing *because* of the suffering, but in the knowledge that through the Holy Spirit, we can go on a path to hope, a path that produces perseverance and character. This is something to rejoice about. But an important factor is that suffering doesn't automatically lead to perseverance, character and hope. It is dependent on our willingness to be open to the leading of the Holy Spirit.

I have seen a number of people go through suffering, and many years later they have not developed perseverance or character, and they have little or no hope. They are stuck in that moment and often consumed by bitterness or unforgiveness. I have also seen many who have gone through horrific suffering but are full of hope for the future. They have received what Paul describes in verse 5: 'God has poured out his love into our hearts by the Holy Spirit, whom he has given us.' Every time we suffer, God invites us to travel that path with Him – a path that leads to hope. It takes a lot of courage to do this, to open yourself up to the work of the Spirit in this way, but the truth of this scripture has been lived out time and time again.

This scripture gave me the courage to hope again when I felt like giving up. God's written word strengthens us. The more we take in, the more we are equipped and changed. The psalmist wrote, 'I have hidden your word in my heart that I might not sin against you' (Psalm 119:11). In his great chapter about leaving behind the old life and taking on the Christian way, Paul encourages the church in Colossae to 'Let the word of Christ dwell in you richly' (Colossians 3:16). When we engage with Scripture there is an encounter that happens that equips us for everyday life and the challenges we face. Something happens, something *sacramental*.

Friends

One thing I have noticed over the years is that when people go through difficult times, there is a tendency to pull away from church. 'Life's pretty tough at the moment so we're going to have a break from church.' This is precisely the opposite of the solution (unless that particular church is causing the suffering!). Right from the start of the Bible we are taught that it is not good for us to be alone. This need for others, for wise counsellors who know us and love us, is magnified in times of suffering. Part of the solution to the problem is to be found in community with our brothers and sisters in our local church. One word of encouragement can change everything.

One Sunday in my 'year of fear' I was at church chatting to my friend Anna. Anna was a doctoral student studying the Eden movement, incredibly wise and a bit of a genius. I was pouring out my woes to her, feeling as if everything was falling apart and I couldn't do it any more and I was pretty rubbish at my job and blah blah blah. Anna looked at me, and with what may sound like a throwaway comment, said, 'Chris, sometimes you've just got to hold your nerve and keep going.' Something happened to me when she said that. It was just like encountering God's word in Scripture. The words went inside me, and made me stronger. It was another sacred moment. Hope flickered in my heart again. We need truth-telling friends who call out the hope inside us. When we face suffering, we should not retreat from church, but embrace it as never before.

Prophetic encouragement

Shortly after the conversation with Esther about giving up, I went off to Holy Island in Northumberland for a three-day retreat. On the way I stopped off in Durham to see a friend, and while I was waiting to see him I decided to go into Durham Cathedral, which was voted Britain's favourite building not long ago. It is a magnificent, awe-inspiring building and a World Heritage Site. I decided to have the whole experience and go up the tower. To get to the top you have to climb 325 steps. Not only that, but they make you pay for the privilege!

As I reached the top I didn't regret it. The views are stunning. As I caught my breath I noticed a dark cloud blowing in. It was a snow cloud, as I soon discovered. The arctic wind swirled around and the snow covered the top of the tower, as people ran for the exit and down the stairs. I started to follow them and then thought, 'Wait a minute, I've just paid for this! I'm going nowhere!' So I pulled my hat down over my face and slouched in a corner until the cloud blew over. The snow was falling so thickly I couldn't even see to the other side of the tower.

After ten freezing cold minutes, the cloud had gone and the sun came out. I stood up and looked out at the views. You could see for miles again, but everything was different. It was all white, sparkling and beautiful, with that magical stillness that only comes when the snow has fallen, when it feels almost holy, and you are compelled to speak in a whisper. In that moment, and totally unexpectedly, God spoke to me. It was a voice in my mind, not an audible voice, that said, 'Chris, this is a picture of your life right now, and if you will just keep going – if you pull your hat down over your face and just sit it out through this storm – the views when it's over will be more beautiful than any you have seen before.' Wow. Thanks, God. A bit of frostbite on my bottom was worth it!

God is so kind, isn't He? And if that wasn't enough, He spoke to me again. A friend of mine invited me to a meeting in a house where a man with a 'prophetic gift' was speaking. I am always a bit nervous around such people. A bit sceptical, but also scared that they might expose the dark secrets of my life to everyone. Not that I've got many, of course, I'm a pretty good lad, all in all... On the way there I was repenting of every sin I could remember committing, and every sin I might possibly have committed or may do in the future. I felt pretty holy when I arrived. I'd show that Prophetic Guy.

After a long and slightly confusing talk, Prophetic Guy offered to pray for me. I put on my holiest look – humble yet pious – and accepted. He asked if there was anything he could pray for, and I told him I had been leading a church for the last six years and it was getting pretty tough. He put his hands on my shoulders and began to pray. I recorded it on my phone in case there was anything good in it.

He said these words to me: 'And so I lay my hands on Chris and say that this is a man that You have shaped over many years, and I thank You for his journey, not just these last six years, but Lord, these last thirteen years, in 1997, where there's been a real journey in his life. And it's like, what he's doing today, so much of it is springing out of what was happening at that time.' It was 1997, thirteen years before, when God had first spoken to me through Mike and all the others about church planting. I looked at Prophetic Guy as if to say *how the heck did you do that*???

And the fact is, he didn't do it. God did it. I realised that God still remembered me. He hadn't moved on to someone else (do you ever feel like that about your friendship with God? Maybe it's just me), He even remembered the year He had said all that stuff to me. He was still with me! It was going to be OK!

I was recently on a trip out with some of the children we work with at LifeCentre. One girl, from an incredibly tough family situation that I can't put into print, sat down next to me, looked in my eyes and said, 'Chris, is it all going to be OK?' I didn't know what to say to her, but I said, 'I really hope so. I really do.' And that is what we all need to hear from God sometimes. *It's going to be OK.* Even in the toughest times, the Christian hope is that eventually, ultimately, it is all going to be OK! Jesus is making all things new! This is the truth that hit me that day as Prophetic Guy nailed it and made me cry. I can have hope, because God knows me, and it's all going to be OK in the end.

It is so important to keep listening out for the whisper of the Spirit when we go through suffering. Sometimes it will be an experience such as that on Durham Cathedral tower, or it may be through a random Prophetic Guy we have never met before or since. We could also be that person for someone else. My friend Anna could never have imagined that she was speaking God's words to me that day. She was just there, being herself, doing her best to help. And God Himself spoke through her and changed me.

The power of hope

It takes a lot of courage to have hope when you are in a dark and difficult place. I had been inspired to persevere, and as a result God was building character in me. But Paul's journey through suffering in Romans 5 culminates in hope, and 'hope does not disappoint us'. When we face one disappointment after another, the easiest thing is to lose all hope. Our vision for what God could do begins to contract, and shrinks to match our difficult experiences. It takes real courage, and sometimes a miracle, to choose to hope.

In the first few years of living in Langworthy, one difficulty was coping with the lawlessness and physical ugliness. God had given us a real love for the place and its people, but wherever you looked there were broken or boarded-up windows covered in graffiti, burned-out cars and litter strewn everywhere. It was a depressing sight. We sometimes did community clean-up days, but they had little lasting effect.

One local lady had an idea to enter Langworthy in the Britain in Bloom competition. This is a national competition to find the most beautiful parts of the UK, and the local community is encouraged to plant flowers and celebrate their town or village. And she wanted Langworthy to compete in this – to have judges come and tour the area and assess how beautiful it was! I thought it was fairly ridiculous, but we got our young people involved and tried to help.

The Langworthy in Bloom team got to work, securing enough funding to buy thousands of hanging baskets – one for every house in the estate – plus huge planters to be attached to fences on the main roads and filled with flowers. And so it was that one week a small army of activists emerged from the rubble and hanging baskets appeared everywhere, filled with vibrant colour and fresh smells. The shopkeepers on either side of Langworthy Road got on board and decorated the front of their shops, and schoolchildren joined in with colourful art and crafts.

I remember being struck by the beauty of it all, but also the incredible vulnerability. All it would take that evening, before the judges came the next day, would be for one teenager (and we knew a few who would enjoy it) to walk up and down each street, turning over each basket on to the ground. I took a lot of pictures so I could remember it before the inevitable destruction occurred.

The next day, something totally unexpected happened. All the flowers and decorations were still there! No one had touched them. The community turned out in force for the judges, and against the odds, Langworthy was awarded first prize in the north-west in its category! Not only that, but it started an annual winning streak that lasted almost a decade.

For us, this was a project that became a parable. We looked around the estate that week. There were still boarded-up houses, broken glass and rubbish. But wherever you looked, there was vibrant colour and stunning beauty. We learned that beauty can be found in ugly places. This project that became a parable taught us that *the flowers of God's kingdom grow in the darkest places.* However dark, however ugly a place or situation is, God is present there, bringing beauty from brokenness, and hope from despair. The Langworthy in Bloom team had incredible courage to hope that such a beautiful, vulnerable initiative could work, but it did. It was almost as if they gave something to the whole estate that meant they could believe again that things could change, to hope again that small and vulnerable and beautiful things could prosper in our estate, and in our lives.

As I was needing hope in my own life, those flowers that outshone the broken glass gave me the courage I needed to carry on. Hope is a precious gift that one human can give to another, and I received it – as did many others in Langworthy – from a lady I barely knew who had a crazy idea that things could change, that hope and creativity could triumph over apathy and destruction.

This parable really sums up everything we have done over nearly two decades here. Incredible, shining beauty in the midst of despair. Flowers that grow and you think they will be destroyed but somehow, against all the odds, they survive and flourish. Even now it feels as though those kingdom flowers could be tipped on to the ground at any moment, but each new day a miracle occurs and they continue to grow. His mercies are new every morning; great is His faithfulness.

Chapter 7
Vulnerability and Success

A few years ago I joined a 'church planting learning community'. It's like a day conference that happens every six months for two years, but 'learning community' sounds more cool and postmodern. Over the course of the two years, we heard from leaders of large churches who told their stories of dramatic church growth, and were encouraged to dream big, and make 'big, hairy, audacious goals'. We learned about 'inflection points' in church growth, multiplication and viral movements. I was quite impressed, if a little taken aback by the grand scale of it all.

But why did I feel so uncomfortable? I'm a pragmatist, and I could see that a lot of this stuff we were learning about was working in real-life situations. Surely I wanted our church to grow, and to see God's kingdom advance? If we want to see a nation changed, won't we need to multiply everything we are doing to reach as many people as possible? If we want to see our estate transformed, won't that require a huge church to disciple everybody? Growing up as a teenager, one of my favourite worship songs was 'History Maker'. It was my generation who bounced up and down singing those words, believing for massive revival in our time. Jesus had thousands of people at some of His meetings, after all.

I could see all the logic in these questions, and something within me still longed to be that 'History Maker'. But I couldn't shake this discomfort with the whole narrative – viral growth, multiplication, audacious goals. I couldn't help thinking there must be another story somewhere, a story we were ignoring – a different definition of success and growth.

It came to a head when we were asked to read the book *Good to Great* by James C Collins. *Good to Great* describes how some companies transition from being good to being great, and why most companies fail to do this. Collins asserts that 'good is the enemy of great',[6] that most companies are content with being good and never make the leap to greatness. I couldn't help wondering how goodness could be the enemy of anything, especially not in the kingdom of God (last year I read *Shrink* by Tim Suttle,[7] where he expresses all these thoughts in a much more powerful and eloquent way than I could do). And besides all that, what is greatness when defined by Jesus? Now I was getting somewhere.

In this chapter I want to explore goodness and greatness, growth and success through the lens of the life and teachings of Jesus. I am not criticising James Collins at all, only questioning the use of business principles such as his in the church.

---

[6] James C Collins, *Good to Great* (New York: Random House, 2001).

[7] Tim Suttle, *Shrink: Faithful Ministry in a Church-Growth Culture* (Grand Rapids,MI: Zondervan, 2014).

YOLO

A few years ago I went into a local high school to talk to some of the pupils about the Easter story. It wasn't easy. I had a cracking talk prepared, even though I do say so myself, but they weren't interested. I changed tack and started asking them questions. Who believes that Jesus rose from the dead? One girl put her hand up and said, 'Yeah, I do.' I was encouraged by this and made the mistake of asking her to say more: 'Yeah, like, it's, like, why would they make that up if it wasn't true?' I nodded encouragingly at the young apologist. 'It's like mermaids, innit? They must be real, fairies too, why would people make them up?' Either she was really cleverly taking me down here, or she was embarrassingly serious. I suspected the latter so offered the question to the rest of the group.

Anyone else? A girl in the corner, chewing gum, feet on the table, puts her hand up. 'I don't think Jesus rose from the dead.' Good. Let's have a debate, then. I ask her how she has come to this conclusion. She replies with a crushing acronym: 'YOLO.' For those of you over a certain age, YOLO stands for You Only Live Once, and for a short while, before it fell out of fashion, it was a rallying cry encouraging young people to live for the moment, to make a bucket list, to have as many experiences as they could, because, well... YOLO.

Even though YOLO is no longer cool, the concept is still a driving force for a generation wanting to find some significance in their lives. Be yourself, be outstanding – you're unique and special – be the best. Go viral. Be on the *X Factor*. Second is nothing. Get better, stronger, faster, reach higher. YOLO!

Nowhere is this more evident than on social media. The buzz of putting up a great picture and watching the likes flood in. Your clever/funny/wise tweet or meme getting retweeted hundreds of times, or your YouTube video going viral. There are celebrities on Twitter who have 'hilarious' banter about who has the most followers. The more followers you have, the more powerful and respected you are.

This kind of school playground talk (mine is bigger than yours!) is even prevalent among Christians. There are some church leaders I know whose conversation starter with other church leaders is always, 'How many have you got now?' How many have you got? That's the kind of question you ask about a stamp collection, or about collecting football stickers, and no way to talk about people!

When we first planted Langworthy Community Church, one leader (who always asked the 'How many?' question) took me under his wing, in a fatherly, slightly patronising manner. After a few months of this, he discovered that in my previous church I used to speak to groups of 800 and more, and I was a regular speaker at some Christian conferences. At this news, he literally got down on his knees and bowed down to me! He told me he now felt insecure with me. I found it incredible how much I had changed in his eyes as he now perceived me very differently. This happened with a number of church leader friends as I got to know them (minus the bowing down). I became important owing to my connections with 'success'.

In my early twenties I was in a band that led worship at lots of the big Christian festivals in the UK. In many places there was a real celebrity culture and hierarchy, depending on the size of stage you had performed on, or the size of the church you were in. There was a trend of trying to climb up a ladder of success. We were interviewed once for a Christian TV channel after leading worship at a well-known festival, and the interviewer said to us, 'This must be a big step up the ladder for you guys, playing at this festival for this amount of people.' I was surprised – we were there to lead some people in worshipping God, not to climb up some ladder – probably a ladder that only has about three rungs with not much of a view at the top! Surely Jesus would be burning the ladder if He was here now? Yet people were wanting us to make music videos and do 'signing sessions'. It was really sad.

I have experienced this in the church too. A man on a gap year in another church came to do a placement in our church. When he first arrived I made him a cup of tea. He was deeply embarrassed that a 'pastor' was making him a brew, when he felt it should be the other way round. On another occasion, I had spoken in front of a big crowd at a Christian youth festival, and our church were also running one of the cafés for the event. That afternoon, I was vacuuming the floor of the café, getting ready to open, when a teenager walking past saw me and came in. She stared for a moment then came over to me and said, 'Excuse me, but are you the guy who was speaking on the main stage this morning?' I said yes and she said, 'So you were up there this morning, and now you're in here, doing the vacuuming! That's so amazing.'

For a while I was overtaken by the moment. I was the Humble Preacher. The Vacuuming Pastor, equally at home on big stages and cleaning up cafés. I deliberately vacuumed near the door for a while longer, in case someone else might notice my humility. I imagined writing my first book, *Humility and How I Achieved It: A Guide to Servanthood in the Kingdom of God*. Sponsored by Dyson and PG Tips.

How have we got to a stage where someone thinks it out of place for a church leader to make someone a cup of tea, or is full of surprised admiration for the fact that a speaker is doing a bit of tidying up? Are we followers of Jesus or not? Didn't He say something about the greatest among us being the servant of all? It should shock us if our leaders are *not* doing the washing-up, or giving someone a lift at their inconvenience, or bringing a meal round for someone in need. Everybody wants to change the world, but nobody wants to do the washing-up.

There is too much emphasis on promoting ourselves and being successful. I saw a study Bible a while ago subtitled 'God's Keys to Personal Success'. When Jesus said, 'If anyone would come after me, he must … take up his cross' (Matthew 16:24), that wasn't the best way of gaining personal success. In fact, it was the quickest way to die. That's the thing with Jesus' kingdom, it doesn't fit our definitions of success, or pander to our versions of the American dream. This is not easy to hear because, if we are honest, most of us would quite like to be outstanding – to leave our mark on the world.

There is something in most of us that wants to be known, to be respected, admired and loved. We have heroes we would love to emulate. As a kid, my hero was Bryan Robson. One day I would be the new Robbo.

Fearless captain of Manchester United and England, a marauding midfielder who could turn a game round single-handedly. I would stand on the Stretford End and watch him lead the team with passion and skill. One day, like Robbo, I would be a great goal-scoring midfielder, I would play for United and England, I would wear number 7, I would even be five foot ten just as he was. Sadly I only reached the dizzy heights of winning the Spring Harvest five-a-side tournament (twice!), only got in my school team when some of the lads started smoking weed and couldn't hack it, and worst of all, I only grew to be five foot nine. One inch away, but it may as well have been a mile. The dream was dead.

Growing up into adulthood as a young Christian, I was a drummer in a band and longed to be able to play like Martin Neil in Kevin Prosch's band (Kevin Prosch was a very influential worship leader in that time). To have that kind of precision and creativity, to know your drumming actually helps people to experience God, and to be pretty cool at the same time, perhaps this was my true calling. My first experience of recording an album confirmed that this was not the case. As I looked through the glass at the sound engineer after my attempt at a ninth take, he had his head in his hands and was gently rocking back and forth. The album artwork also revealed another issue: I am not cool. Drumming will remain a nice hobby.

Some of my friends and I had an idea to run some youth meetings for Christians in Greater Manchester. These monthly events gathered quite a good crowd, and as numbers grew to around 200, I imagined us as the Soul Survivor of the north. Perhaps I could become a world-class speaker and host meetings like Mike Pilavachi, and people would laugh at my jokes, and invitations to preach around the world would flood in. Or maybe that was the peak of what God wanted for those meetings, and they would fizzle out as we tried to keep them going longer than we should have? We didn't become the Soul Survivor of the north, and I certainly didn't become the next Mike Pilavachi, as I had secretly hoped.

Then, thirteen years ago, we started a church. I joined my learning community and read the great stories of churches that started out in a front room and within two years were thousands strong. I also heard people tell me that if you start a church in an inner-city estate, it's really hard work and it won't grow. I was confident we would buck that trend. I even read books about church-planting movements where churches rapidly multiplied around whole regions, and I imagined myself leading such a movement with churches planted all over the north-west of England. I would be the Bill Hybels of the inner-city church. (I'm not the Bill Hybels of the inner-city church, by the way.)

We have seen wonderful things happen and many lives changed and an estate transformed in the last eighteen years, but if you turn up on a Sunday, you won't be impressed. Bill Hybels has Willow Creek church, we meet in Willow Tree school, but that's the only similarity. Yesterday there were thirty of us worshipping together. The time before that when I was there, 100 came. We eat food together and talk about Jesus. It's not big or flashy or impressive at all. But I love it.

I just finished studying for an MA in theology. On Thursday I'm presenting a paper at an academic conference. I now have theological heroes to go with my football/drumming/church heroes. What can I learn from my life so far, when I read about Hauerwas, Moltmann, and Tom Wright, and imagine writing books like theirs and spending my life studying and teaching as they do? I have written myself a memo:

> Chris, you're not going to be the next Tom Wright. You're not that clever. Also, you're not charismatic and funny like Mike Pilavachi. You can't write like Don Miller. You can't play football like Bryan Robson. You can't drum like Martin Neil. You are never going to lead a church like Bill Hybels does. And that is actually OK. You are ordinary old Chris Lane. You wear glasses that are not as cool as Rob Bell's. And you can't write as well as him either.
>
> Even if you put one sentence on a line, like this.
>
> Chris, you are not cool, you are going bald and you're too hairy and you are an ordinary bloke doing your best to be a good husband, a good dad and a good friend and church leader. Maybe God's trying to tell you to be yourself, and just maybe you are starting to do that after forty-one years of trying to be extraordinary. Maybe the best thing you can do is to love the next person you meet, to listen to them, to hear what God might be saying to them, and to pray for them. Then move on to the next person. And perhaps God might want you not to stand out from the

crowd but just be OK at everything, and that might just work out well for you. Perhaps it's more important that you spent five days just having fun with the kids last week and hardly picking up your phone/iPad/PC, than the fact that this week you're doing six preaches and that might make you feel important? Maybe having thirty or 100 people come to a Sunday meeting shouldn't affect your morale so much? Is it not more important that each of those people who did come felt a connection with God and felt loved by His people?

I'm part of a generation who were taught to look for the big bang, to pray for revival, to change the world, to make a bucket list and do it all on our gap years, to live life to the max – to be outstanding and exceptional and be the best – but by definition only a tiny number of people will be outstanding. The rest of us need to get on with being ourselves, loving the people who we come into contact with, serving others, not waiting for our big break but getting on with living as ordinary people in ordinary time, believing in an extraordinary God.

In his book *¡Gracias!*, Henri Nouwen gives this stunning challenge:

> My own desire to be useful, to do something significant, or to be part of some impressive project is so strong that soon my time is taken up by meetings, conferences, study groups, and workshops that prevent me from walking the streets. It is difficult not to have plans, not to organise people around an urgent cause, and not

to feel that you are working directly for social progress. But I wonder more and more if the first thing shouldn't be to know people by name, to eat and drink with them, to listen to their stories and tell your own, and to let them know with words, handshakes and hugs that you do not simply like them, but truly love them.[8]

Jesus tells us a number of hard truths about greatness. When James and John came to Him asking if they could sit at His right and left when He became King, He told the disciples, 'You know that those who are regarded as rulers of the Gentiles lord it over them, and their high officials exercise authority over them. Not so with you. Instead, whoever wants to become great among you must be your servant, and whoever wants to be first must be slave of all. For even the Son of Man did not come to be served, but to serve, and to give his life as a ransom for many' (Mark 10:42-45).

Success and greatness in Jesus' kingdom starts with a downwards path – to wash people's feet, to love your enemies and take the place of least honour. 'If anyone would come after me, he must deny himself and take up his cross daily and follow me. For whoever wants to save his life will lose it, but whoever loses his life for me will save it' (Luke 9:23-24). Jesus turns everything on its head – 'the last will be first, and the first will be last' (Matthew 20:16).

---

[8] Henry Nouwen, ¡Gracias! A Latin American Journal (New York: Orbis Books, 2005), pp 147-148.

This doesn't sound like a great recipe for success or growth! Jesus doesn't have great church growth techniques, or 'ten lifestyle hacks to make you totally holy' as BuzzFeed might put it today. Sometimes he seems determined to reduce the crowds, as in John 6 when He starts telling the crowds they have to eat His flesh and drink His blood, and many leave, and He is only left with the disciples who decide to stay as they have nowhere else to go! In fact at the end, even the eleven had deserted Him and He was left with His mum and a small group of friends, never having had His own Christian TV channel, never having left His own country, and having been executed after only three years of public ministry. Not the best success story. And yet this man, His story and His followers would utterly transform the world forever.

Remember the flowers in the previous chapter? They brought such hope and beauty into an ugly, dark place, and yet they were incredibly vulnerable. This is what God did in the incarnation of Jesus. The eternal Son of God became a vulnerable baby, born in dangerous circumstances to a teenage girl in a borrowed room. And then Jesus calls His followers to a similar vulnerability:

> At that time the disciples came to Jesus and asked, 'Who, then, is the greatest in the kingdom of heaven?' He called a little child to him, and placed the child among them. And he said: 'Truly I tell you, unless you change and become like little children, you will never enter the kingdom of heaven. Therefore, whoever takes the lowly

position of this child is the greatest in the kingdom of heaven.'
Matthew 18:1-4 (NIV 2011)

Unless we change and become like little children, we will never enter the kingdom of heaven! This seems ridiculous to us now, but even more so for Jesus' original listeners. Recently I was in IKEA and saw a sign saying, 'Children are the most important people in the world'. This is the opposite to Jesus' day, when children were of little value. They couldn't produce income, they were often ill and many never made it to adulthood. Jesus is calling His followers to become weak, unimportant and vulnerable. This is not just a bit of advice, but a condition of entering the kingdom. Jesus' definition of greatness is the polar opposite to how the world, and most of the Church, define it. We need to repent and change, and become like little children as Jesus commands.

Healthy things grow?

Finally in this chapter, I want to explore the idea that is often mentioned in church leadership conferences, the statement that 'healthy things grow and reproduce'. As with most maxims, there is truth in this. When I was a child, I grew as any healthy young boy should. Those who didn't grow were referred to the doctor to discover what was wrong. However, in my late teens, for no reasons of ill health, I stopped growing. I had reached my optimum height.

Now, there have been times since then that I have grown. I have not grown upwards, but outwards. The growth in recent years has all been unhealthy growth, coinciding with supermarkets selling salted caramel ice cream for half price. A year or two ago I stood on a Wii Fit board, and while it was weighing me it said, 'Hello Chris, I've not seen you for 547 days! You've got bigger – do you have trouble walking?' That was the day I got rid of the Wii and bought an Xbox. But the growth I had experienced was an unhealthy, self-indulgent growth that was damaging my body.

This is also the case with reproduction. Esther and I are parents of three great kids, but there will come a time when we will be unable to produce any more, not because we are unhealthy but because it is just a new stage in our lives.

Living things also grow at different rates depending on environment. The more space and nutrients a tree has, the bigger it will grow. Depending on where a church is planted, it will grow to different sizes and in different ways.

Let's see it from another angle. There are many things that grow and reproduce rapidly that are not healthy. Bacteria are one example. Or take a disease such as cancer. It grows and multiplies, but its growth destroys and kills the rest of the body. I have seen some churches rapidly grow, but virtually all the growth has come at the expense of other churches, taking all their key people and causing some to close down altogether. If we are a body, we need to ensure that, in our pursuit of greatness, multiplication and growth, we don't do serious damage to the rest of the body of Christ. When we planted our church, I did my best to discourage people from other churches in the area coming to join us for this reason. We wanted to grow with people who were not in a church already.

I was giving a talk recently on this subject and a guy stopped me and said, 'But if it isn't about numbers, how do we measure success?' He had got straight to the heart of the issue. How might Jesus answer? I wonder if He might say that success is being faithful to Him? As He lived His life doing only what He saw the Father doing, so must we. Often the Father will lead us into insignificance and difficult places. Sometimes He might lead us into positions of prominence where we are 'known' by many people. But if we seek that, it can only lead to disaster.

A couple of times in my life, I have had the opportunity to go on a different path from the one I am on now. One would have led to a career and the money that goes with that, and the other would have led to more prominence in Christian circles. Both times I had to bring it to God and obey what He told me to do. It's the only way to go. Eugene Peterson used Nietzsche's phrase 'A long obedience in the same direction'[9] to summarise the kind of life Jesus calls us to. Not always pursuing the next place and the next adrenaline rush, but serving faithfully, often in the shadows, seeing God's kingdom come and His will being done.

Christian leadership needs a huge overhaul. We need to stop trying to climb a ladder of success, stop trying to build our own brand, or manufacture church growth in a way akin to an athlete using steroids. It looks great, but ultimately it destroys the body. It destroys Jesus' body.

---

[9] E H Peterson, *A Long Obedience in the Same Direction: Discipleship in an Instant Society* (Downers Grove, IL: Intervarsity Press, 2000).

Instead of stronger, bigger, faster, greater, how about slower, deeper, lower, and maybe even smaller?

Imagine if a new generation of Christian leaders actually took the words of Jesus seriously. If we lived out a different story to the world, instead of buying into everything on the market. If we valued goodness over greatness. As I said earlier, you might find young, talented musicians, instead of trying to become a 'worship pastor' at a megachurch, devoting decades of their lives to investing in disadvantaged young people in a forgotten estate, giving them value and showing them how to meet God through music. You might find a change in the number of people 'feeling called' to the most exciting areas of the country and to the big, impressive churches, and instead pioneering radical new forms of church in inner-city and rural communities, or among asylum seekers and other marginalised groups.

Perhaps our churches might start to reflect the first Jesus communities who broke bread and broke all the social norms of the day, sharing life with the down-and-outs and the hated ones, the smelly people and the weirdos. And that would be truly beautiful. To see those kingdom flowers growing all across our nation as God's people simply love and serve where the need is greatest – surely we will see wonderful things happen. This is the worship God requires:

> To loose the chains of injustice,
> and untie the cords of the yoke,
> to set the oppressed free
> and break every yoke?
> Is it not to share your food with the hungry

and to provide the poor wanderer with shelter –
when you see the naked, to clothe him,
and not to turn away from your own flesh and
blood?
Then your light will break forth like the dawn,
and your healing will quickly appear.
Isaiah 58:6-8

And perhaps, like the apostle Paul, we will catch a vision of Jesus so compelling that we consider all the impressive statistics about growth and greatness to be like dung compared to the surpassing greatness of knowing Christ Jesus our Lord (Philippians 3:8)? This is my prayer.

Chapter 8
Prayer and Presence

Langworthy had hit rock bottom in the mid 1990s. During that time, when any sensible person wouldn't walk around there, and tradespeople often refused to work there owing to the risk of damage to their cars, some good friends of ours called Dave and Karen lived in the heart of the estate, with their young daughter. They had moved into the area in 1992, and their daughter, Elizabeth, was born the next year. Within three years, Langworthy descended quickly into lawless chaos. Dave and Karen were committed to a life of prayer, but it wasn't easy for anyone to survive in Langworthy in those days. Half of the houses on their street had been abandoned – including either side of their house, causing damp – and one of the notorious gangs used to hang out just opposite their house. Their daughter struggled with her health, partly as a result of the living conditions. During their years in that house, a friend of theirs would ring them every night to ask how he could pray for them. These prayers sustained the family against seemingly impossible odds.

Another consequence of the decline of the estate was a crash in property prices, and houses bought for £30,000 a few years earlier were now being sold at £5,000 or less. This left many, including Dave and his family, in serious financial difficulty. As Dave and Karen prayed over the estate, spending many hours over the years prayer walking around the streets of Langworthy, God began to speak to them about their future and the future of the estate. Dave sensed that his time in Langworthy was coming to an end, but that God was giving him three promises. Firstly, that when the family moved out, some Christians would move into their house. Secondly, at the same time, a group of Christians would move en masse into the streets around theirs. And finally, that they would not be left in any debt (which would require a financial miracle of around £20,000).

In 1999, the year we moved into Langworthy to start the Eden Salford Project, Dave and the family left Langworthy. Not only did my friends James and Hayley move into their house, but a team of twenty-eight Christians moved into the streets surrounding their street, and their debt was paid off! We were in no doubt that God had brought us here. The other thing that was very clear was that we were surfing on a great wave of prayer that had gone before us. Some older folk from the church came to us that year to tell us that they had lived in Langworthy for many years, and had prayed again and again for God to move in the estate. We didn't need to create a new movement, only to join in with what God was stirring in response to those faithful men and women of God who had fasted and prayed and believed for a move of God, often against all the odds and in defiance of the decline they were seeing with their eyes.

Prayer undergirds all we do, and we cannot be effective without it. In Salford and across Greater Manchester and beyond, there was a significant inter-church prayer movement in the years leading up to the start of our work in Langworthy. Churches came together from all over the city in united prayer, blessing each other and crying out for God to pour out the Holy Spirit on the Church and in society. We saw God answer these prayers and many young people in our church and in churches all over Salford were set on fire with a passion for Jesus and for prayer. As a remarkable move of God spread around the Salford churches in the mid 1990s, there were lots of prophecies about needing to take this to the streets, that it couldn't be contained in the church buildings. We took this literally and would often leave the meetings at the end and all walk down the hill around the streets of Langworthy, calling out to God to move in power. There was such passion in the intercession of that time, and I am convinced that it created a spiritual momentum that enabled Eden and Langworthy Community Church to be birthed, and then to have an impact on the community in the way we have done so far.

It is a combination of prayer and mission that often brings a breakthrough. But we don't always realise that the wonderful things we see God do are actually a direct result of the prayers and prophetic insights of people who prayed many years before. One vision I have already referred to, that was seen by three different people during that move of God in the mid 1990s, was a picture of a river (water is often involved in such charismatic visions!) that flowed out of Mount Chapel and down the middle of Langworthy Road. The river gave life to many willow trees that were planted on either side of the river, and the trees grew strong, and their leaves provided healing to people.

We imagined that we were those willow trees flowing along the river out of Mount Chapel, planted in the estate, providing healing for the people. Then years later the council declared Langworthy a 'renewal area'. We thought this sounded great! Part of the renewal was that they knocked down some of the old terraced blocks, including our friend Dave's house, to make way for a new primary school to be built. Letters were sent to the residents to ask for a vote on the name of the new school. One of the four suggestions was Eden School! But the one they voted for was Willow Tree Primary School. When the decision was made we instantly thought of those prophetic visions of the willow trees growing and bringing healing to the community. When the school opened, it was agreed that Langworthy Community Church could meet there on Sundays, and we have done ever since. The school hall where we worship each week stands on the same location where Dave's house once stood, where Dave and Karen would pray day after day, year after year for God to break through here. Even the place we worship is an answer to prayer!

One thing we as a church have felt God saying in the last year or two is that for what He wants to do next, we need a fresh prayer movement. It is almost as if the momentum created in the 1990s has taken us to this point, but we need to prepare ourselves again for the next stage. We have added a second weekly prayer meeting, and begun to call the church to fasting again, and when we renovated the LifeCentre we made sure there was one room that was a dedicated prayer room – a physical way of highlighting the centrality of prayer in everything we do. Prayer is a way that God includes us in His work in the world. It has the effect of changing us as much as it changes the circumstances around us. We need to remember that some of our prayers will not be answered for a generation, but we sow and believe and trust that God is faithful.

One thing we pray for is an open heaven over Langworthy. This is a bit of Christian jargon, so I will try to explain what I mean. Inner-city estates are tough, and workers often feel the need to escape to somewhere 'nicer' in order to recuperate and hear from God. Our prayer has been that people would begin to come to Langworthy to meet with God and encounter the Holy Spirit. It can happen. In another part of Salford, a friend of ours is pioneering inner-city retreats, where people come to her estate to receive prayer and encounter God. It is already happening. The tough places of our country can become places like Bethel, where in the Old Testament Jacob saw heaven touching earth, and subsequently it was regarded as a place to pray and hear from God. Prayer can change the spiritual atmosphere of a place. People who return to Langworthy after a number of years often tell us that it 'feels different' – brighter, friendlier, somehow *easier* and more welcoming. Prayer changes things.

Prayer often changes things when it is accompanied by an experience of the presence of God. We have found repeatedly that the most powerful moments of change in people's lives have been when they have experienced God's presence, in all kinds of places. Only last week a new family came along to church for the first time, and as we worshipped using songs, the mum began to cry gently. She was experiencing God's love in her life. We have been running a lifestyle course with some biblical content, and at the end of each session we spend time in prayer. Recently there was a really strong sense of the Holy Spirit in the room. A lady who had come along for the first time told us later that she had been going through some really difficult times, but that during those five minutes of prayer she had experienced total peace for the first time in many years. We were able to share with her about the peace that comes from Jesus.

The presence of God is the most wonderful thing. I often find myself in some meeting or other, a bit tired and perhaps slightly bored, when suddenly I sense the presence of God. In that moment everything changes. Suddenly, instead of thinking about how uncomfortable my chair is, or what I'm going to have for dinner, there is no place in the world I would rather be. I feel as though I could stay there forever and I don't care at all about food or my own needs. All I can think of is how I want everyone else to experience this too because it is so amazing!

Jesus promised He would always be with us. In fact Christians worship Jesus as *Immanuel*, which means God is with us. This is one of the great truths of the Bible – God with us. As Psalm 23 tells us, even though we walk through the valley of the shadow of death, we will fear no evil, for He is with us. When God calls Moses, and Moses is looking for some support or affirmation ('Who am I …?', Exodus 3:11). God doesn't give him an encouraging compliment but simply says, 'I will be with you' (Exodus 3:12). That is enough. That is ultimately what we all need to know, that He is with us. The God who created heaven and earth is with us. He is our cloud by day and fire by night. He is the unseen guest at our dinner tables. He brings us peace beyond our understanding.

God's presence is not restricted to emotional worship meetings with beautiful music and moving stories. One guy who had been along to church once or twice came to one of our live music nights. The evenings are not overtly evangelistic, just a place for people to connect who are into live music. He sat there listening to various hits from across the decades, and came to talk to me at the end. 'Chris, I've been sat here for the last hour with this strange feeling, and I've realised what it is. I'm happy! I've not felt this for years! You know on Sunday you were saying that you can have an experience with God? Well, that's just happened to me sitting on that stool!' No one had prayed for him and there was no worship music or preaching, just the love of God reaching out to a guy who needed him. His presence is wonderful. We had been praying for years for people to sense the presence of God when they were in the LifeCentre, and over the last year or so we have seen it happen on a number of occasions, often when we least expect it. One lady came in to ask for help recently, but as soon as she walked in she stopped and said, 'Something is different in here. I feel safe for the first time in ages. I feel secure. Why is that?'

On another occasion, a few of us were sitting in a front room having a meal together when we started to chat about things God had been saying to us. All of a sudden the atmosphere in the room changed. The conversation paused briefly as we took it in. One friend, a teenager who was new to church, spoke first. 'He's 'ere, isn't He? God's here.' It was exactly the same sense of wonder, goodness and holiness that I've experienced so many times in big worship meetings. Only this time in a front room. One person started to cry, and we saw similar manifestations of the Holy Spirit to those we had seen in meetings, but around a table in a house, with no background music.

For the last two years we have set up a prayer room for a week in our local school, and in the second year a Year 4 girl literally ran into the room with delight on her face, saying, 'I've been looking forward to this all year!' The teachers at the school all commented that the children were much calmer when they emerged from their hour in the prayer room. This is the peace that comes from God.

Prayer is linked to the presence of God. God loves to answer our prayers for His presence. Luke 3 tells us that Jesus was praying when the Spirit descended on Him at His baptism. The Holy Spirit came to a prayer meeting on the day of Pentecost. The Wesley brothers and George Whitefield, who were preachers and revivalists in the eighteenth century, were in an all-night prayer meeting on 1st January 1739, when the Holy Spirit came and empowered them for their world-influencing ministries. It appears that all the great revivals throughout Church history have been birthed by, and sustained in, fervent prayer. One of the reasons we love inviting people to experience prayer rooms is that combination of prayer and the presence of God. Once people experience His presence, nothing else will satisfy. For all the people we have taken to the Soul Survivor events, the one thing they enjoy most are the times of prayer ministry where they experience God's presence.

Prayer with fasting is also a powerful practice. Years ago my brother and I went to a conference really desperate to meet with God. A guy stood up to preach and called the room to commit to a forty-day fast of no food and only drinking water. Andrew and I were two of the first to stand and commit to it. We were up for anything that would help us experience more of God. As the time of the fast got closer, we started to get scared, and also admitted that God hadn't actually told us to do it; we just thought it would be cool. Now we realised we might die. And we had a few things we wanted to do with our lives before we died. So we slightly changed the nature of the fast to a Daniel-style fast of only eating fruit and veg. In a major step for me, I pledged to go without cheese and crisps for the whole forty days!

I imagined that this fast would launch us into full-blown revival, perhaps leading to an international revival ministry with my own plane and a programme on Christian TV. It didn't. It was pretty hard and most of my journal for the forty days contains big questions such as 'Where is God? Why can't I hear from him?' However, at the end of the forty days, a few of us got together in my front room to pray. I was really fed up and a bit embarrassed that I hadn't had any incredible experiences, no prophetic dreams or angelic visitations. Mainly I just had a funny stomach from a dramatic change of diet.

In that room at the end of the forty days of fasting, we started to pray. We were lethargic and not particularly full of faith. Within a couple of minutes the room fell silent as we all sensed that God was in the room. This sense was so holy I got on my knees and didn't dare to move. For three hours, a room full of teenagers and young adults sat completely still in awe and wonder at God being *with us.* There was an extra level of awe and the sense of God's love and holiness that seems only to accompany prayer with fasting. It seems to bring a special breakthrough. I hate fasting, so would prefer this not to be true, but it is!

In Matthew 17:21 and Mark 9:29, the disciples have struggled and failed to free a boy from a demon that was oppressing him. Jesus then frees the boy from the demon and rebukes the disciples, telling them 'this kind can come out only by prayer and fasting'. There is some debate about this phrase because it isn't found in all the earliest Greek manuscripts, but it does appear that Jesus and His followers believed there was an added power to prayer when combined with fasting. Luke makes a point of telling us that Jesus was *filled* with Holy Spirit when He went into the desert to begin His forty-day fast, but He emerged from the fast in the *power* of the Holy Spirit. In fasting we are able to break through in prayer in major ways.

One key to welcoming God's presence among us is a passage in Paul's first letter to the Thessalonians. In chapter 5, Paul gives a concise list of instructions for the Church in the way of following Jesus:

> Now we ask you, brothers and sisters, to acknowledge those who work hard among you, who care for you in the Lord and who admonish you. Hold them in the highest regard in love because of their work. Live in peace with each other. And we urge you, brothers and sisters, warn those who are idle and disruptive, encourage the disheartened, help the weak, be

patient with everyone. Make sure that nobody pays back wrong for wrong, but always strive to do what is good for each other and for everyone else. Rejoice always, pray continually, give thanks in all circumstances; for this is God's will for you in Christ Jesus. Do not quench the Spirit. Do not treat prophecies with contempt but test them all; hold on to what is good, reject every kind of evil.

1 Thessalonians 5:12-22 (NIV 2011)

As with his instructions on the use of gifts of the Holy Spirit in 1 Corinthians 12–14, Paul links our treatment of each other with the experience of the Spirit. In Corinth, the church were obsessed with spiritual power but were involved in all kinds of immorality and injustice. In the middle of his two great chapters on spiritual gifts, there is the famous chapter on love. We can speak in the tongues of men and angels, but if we don't have love, we have nothing. We could have the gift of prophecy and fathom all kinds of mysteries and knowledge, but without love, our lives are an empty noise, like a clanging cymbal. Love for each other must be at the heart of any use of the powerful gifts of the Spirit, and love is key to our experience of God's presence among us.

Here in Thessalonians, Paul again challenges the church in their treatment of each other, especially their weaker members. He reminds them to be thankful always, and to rejoice always, as well as challenging them to 'pray without ceasing' (NRSV). Immediately after this line he says, 'Do not quench the Spirit. Do not treat prophecies with contempt'.

Instructing the people *not* to quench the Spirit, or 'put out the Spirit's fire' as some translations have it (for example, ISV), clearly implies that it is possible to do this. How is it done? I was at a conference many years ago when one of the leaders seemed to have a gift for stopping the worship and prayer just as it seemed that God was really moving, and we jokingly nicknamed him 'the Quencher'. But we can be quenchers too! When we treat people badly, when we are not thankful, when we go after power rather than love, when we hold bitterness in our hearts towards others, in all these things we can quench the Spirit.

When I first discovered that the gifts of the Spirit were for today, it was an amazing thing for me. I was scared at first, coming from a background that didn't believe in such things. My youth leader invited me to an event called Full Gospel Businessmen's Fellowship International. A pretty long title, if you ask me. I went along and it was full of large men in suits who hugged each other. In the Brethren church we didn't hug, we shook hands, and the firmer your handshake the holier you were. Some of the wise Brethren elders would nearly break your knuckles if you let them. I was disturbed by the FGB big men, and their hugs and their loudness. 'PRAISE THE LORD, HALLELUJAH' they would shout at each other and at God.

Then the meeting started and they all began to sing and shout in what sounded like gobbledygook. I looked down, embarrassed, and saw on the table a card with cartoon picture on it. This was designed to explain to newcomers like me what was going on. One cartoon had a picture of a man with a speech bubble with nonsense words in it, with the caption 'speaking in tongues'. So that explained that to me. The cartoon next to it had a picture of someone falling to the ground, as if dead. The caption there said 'being slain in the Spirit'. I had no clue what this meant, but was now completely terrified that I was about to be slain. If it was supposed to helpful and welcoming, this cartoon made me want to run!

Despite my fears, and the loud, hugging men, I sensed something there that I wanted, something I needed. The seed planted that day led me at one point to become one of those conference-hoppers – going round from conference to conference seeking out an experience of the Holy Spirit. These events all had names such as Seek the Fire, Fresh Wind or River People. Sometimes I couldn't remember if we were jumping in the river or calling down fire, or asking for some wind (I had quite enough wind), but I was up for any of it if it involved experiencing God's wonderful presence. Everyone was prophesying revival, big things happening, a mighty move of God.

After a few years I began to tire of this. I began to be cynical of this pursuit of God. Or more accurately, of the pursuit of experiences. But the problem with cynicism is that it's like poison. Once it gets a hold of you, it brings you down. It affects every part of your life. And worst of all, it quenches the Holy Spirit. Don't get me wrong, there is a place for a healthy scepticism. In our passage in Thessalonians, Paul actually tells us to test prophecies. But he also tells us not to treat them with contempt. I was so cynical. Whenever I heard someone give a prophetic word I would think, 'Oh, really? Well, let's see, shall we?' I was treating them with contempt, and quenching the Spirit.

I needed to repent. If I am called to be like a little child, part of that is repenting of my cynical attitudes about people and about God's work, and recovering some innocence. Not to assume I know better than others. Not to instantly think, 'Flip, I've heard that one before, and it never happens. Another wildly optimistic prophetic word.' To always think the best of others, and to 'always strive to do what is good for each other and for everyone else', and value others above myself, as Paul commands in 1 Thessalonians 5:15.

Just recently, a friend of mine visited a big Christian festival with me for the day. He was instantly cynical of it all, saying it was all hype, and just for middle-class people and other easy targets. I found myself nodding along – there is always some truth in such critiques – but then stopped myself. I was returning to an unhealthy cynicism. I remembered Paul's instructions to be thankful, and reminded myself of all the times I had experienced literally life-changing moments in those big, noisy meetings. I remembered how most of what I am doing now for God, I was inspired to do so through a talk I had heard there, or a prophetic word I had been given. I still have tear-stained bits of paper I had written in those meetings while the band played, where I sensed God calling me to move into Langworthy, to plant a church, to quit my job and trust Him for money.

In thankfulness, we are able to overcome cynicism. Thankfulness helps us to return to innocence and allows the Spirit to work in us again. Don't quench the Spirit. Don't put out the Spirit's fire. Don't treat prophecies with contempt. Be thankful.

Chapter 9
Friendship and Community

Looking through the big story of the Bible and at the people God used to change the world, one thing that always strikes me is that God doesn't just call individuals, but communities. It starts with Adam, and it wasn't good for him to be alone. There is a longing within all of us to be part of a community. The story of Israel begins with Abram, but not just him; Sarah, too; and not just that couple, but also their descendants. God didn't call out a person, but a people.

Moses didn't rescue the people from Egypt on his own – Miriam and Aaron were equally part of that leadership team in the Exodus story. Deborah probably could have done it on her own, but included Barak and others. King David had Jonathan, and his mighty men. Jesus gathered His disciples, and then sent them out in pairs, never on their own. The Holy Spirit was poured out at Pentecost on a whole community, igniting and launching a church, not Simon Peter International Revival Ministries.

In the same way, God calls us into community. His mission is always carried out through a people, not just a person. The gospel is about a Person, but it is lived out by a people. Some of my good friends in recent years have become disillusioned by their experiences of the Church.

Leaders have let them down, structures have proven destructive, and they have decided to 'be church' and not attend a particular local church any more. Some say to me that they meet around a pub table regularly with like-minded friends and study the Bible, and that is church for them. Others say they get all they need in their own homes, listening to podcasts of great preachers and worship albums.

I have no doubt in the sincerity of my friends who live like this, nor do I doubt their love for Jesus. My concerns are that they are missing out on the full experience of church community. As I said earlier, one thing I love when I look round the room when our church gathers together is the thought that these people would *never* be in a room together if it wasn't for a miracle! They would never choose to hang out with each other, if it wasn't for Jesus. The Church is truly a countercultural miracle. In a world of social media echo chambers where all our friends think, say and share the same things and block people with different opinions, the Church gathers all kinds of people into one room to share bread and wine, to try to work out how to love each other in the midst of all our differences.

Alcoholics sit next to PhD students, lonely old people read stories to young kids with ADHD, people who love singing songs pour out their hearts alongside friends who hate singing. The problem with church being around a pub table is that the pub table is quite small and exclusive, and we usually fill it with people who look like us, think like us and back up most of our opinions. Church at its most beautiful is a big family with all kinds of odd-bods in it. The weird uncle, the eccentric great-auntie and those cousins who always leave a mess. The awkward Dad jokes, Grandad's wind, and the baby who never stops crying; your brother who always winds you up. But they're all family, and so you come together and try to make it work. They don't stop being family because they smell, offend you or disagree with you.

Sitting at home listening to your favourite preacher on a podcast is not church. Church should be a miracle every time it gathers. It should include people who make it really hard for you to obey Jesus' teachings (love your neighbour, love your enemies, pray for those who persecute you). Ultimately, church can be a glimpse of the kingdom that is coming. All kinds of random people, especially the ones no one else likes, trying to work out how to love each other, all coming round the table, all acknowledging their need for Jesus, all eating from the same loaf of bread and drinking from the same cup. Visitors to our churches should be amazed at how diverse we are – what are all these people doing in the same room? We need to be regularly worshipping with people who think, look and smell differently to us. Our churches should be glimpses of Jesus' kingdom, where forgiveness is common, where we go the extra mile for people we don't like, where grace is abundant.

There is a cost to living like this. Jesus gathered a group of people who would never have come together otherwise – tax collectors and Zealots on the same team! It must have been incredibly difficult at times. Judas had been casting out demons and healing the sick with the other eleven, but he betrayed Jesus at the last and the others fled too. When we invest and give our lives to a diverse community, we are taking a risk, and it is not easy.

A few years ago a woman came to me who had been a part of my youth group. She had lost her job, been kicked out of her house and was facing a criminal trial for drug possession. She asked me if I could help. I was tired and stressed at the time and my first thought was, 'No, and I'm not even sure if God can help either!' I didn't say that, obviously. She also had a huge problem with compulsive lying, often not realising herself what was true or untrue. She had lied to me many times in the past, so I decided I would try to help, but also try to treat her as a client, and not get emotionally involved.

The problem with being a Christian is that it is really hard not to get emotionally involved! You're supposed to love everyone, and the Holy Spirit living inside you constantly pushes you to love people, giving you compassion for them. I didn't want any compassion or love for her! I didn't want to hope she could change, because I didn't want the crushing disappointment when she would let me down. As the months went by we became friends again, and she began to change for the better. She was such a brilliant person when she wasn't stoned, incredibly thoughtful, caring and helpful.

I wish this story had a great ending and she is now one of the leaders of our church. She isn't. She started selling weed to some of our young people, and things went downhill from there. And she took a piece of me when she left, again. It is really tough trying to live out the teachings of Jesus in this way, but I can't see an alternative in the Bible.

I could tell a number of stories like that – people who joined us, were incredibly demanding and intense, gave us some hope they would change, then left suddenly, either without a goodbye or sometimes leaving a trail of destruction in their wake. It can put you off investing in people, because you know they will hurt you, but the alternative – shutting yourself off emotionally – is worse. The truth is that God also brings wonderful people into your life, and we could miss them if we are closed and distrustful in our relationships. We need to be open to the wonder of friendship.

One of the best things about the work I do is that I get to work with some amazing people, who are my closest friends. I have already told you about some of them, but when I look back I can see that God has always provided the right people at the right time. When I started out leading a church, one leader had advised me not to become close friends with anyone in my congregation, as it could make life too awkward and people would think I had favourites. I did not take this advice! For a start, I simply can't work that way, given my personality, but I also don't think it reflects the example of Jesus. He quite clearly had some people with whom He spent more time, and shared more of His life, than others. I don't think this was just some clever leadership strategy (investing in the future leaders), but the natural human propensity towards deep friendship with a small group.

Surely, if we in churches can't be friends, what are we modelling to people? We should be living out what true friendship looks like. And God brings us the people we need. It is my privilege to lead the church with my closest friend – my brother – and another great friend who manages our LifeCentre, Beth. Beth and her husband, Dave, felt God calling them to move to Salford and first got in touch with me via email. They were living in leafy Chippenham in Wiltshire at the time, and Beth had recently graduated from Cambridge University. Moving to inner-city Salford was not the career choice of any of her high-flying fellow graduates! But Beth and Dave came to visit us to see if it was the right move for them.

I tend to try to put Christians off who are thinking of joining LCC, as we have always been a church for people in our estate who don't know Jesus yet. So I told them about every other church in the area and how great they all were. But they still seemed to want to visit us. Beth had been inspired to move to Salford after hearing Andy Hawthorne preach about Eden at a Christian conference. Dave was nervous about coming and prayed that he would know someone at the service. By apparent complete coincidence, the first person Dave saw when he came in was a guy he had met on a YFC gap year. Not only that, but Andy Hawthorne was the preacher that day! They moved a few months later and have been key leaders and pioneers and dear friends ever since. God provides for us.

Another couple who responded to this call were Martin and Yvonne. Their daughter Angie was part of the Eden Salford team, and they were visiting on that first Easter meal when we had launched the church. I was twenty-eight when we planted LCC, and was one of the oldest people even then! Martin and Yvonne were a couple of decades ahead of us. As a very young group of church planters not attached to any denomination, we often found ourselves out of our depth. We had a great friendship with a church in Manchester whose leader, Andrew Belfield, was a mentor to me and gave invaluable help and advice to us, as he still does to this day. But we had no one within the congregation who could provide us with the wisdom and the sense of safety and security that only come with age and maturity.

Yvonne was from a spiritualist background. She attended a C of E church but her parents also took her along to the spiritualist church. It was recognised that she could 'pick up the spirits', but she was increasingly drawn to Christianity, and in her teens experienced a baptism in the Holy Spirit. While her parents held séances downstairs, she would stay in her room and pray! One day she was suddenly consumed by fear and plunged into depression, which lasted eleven years, even after she met and married Martin, a local Sunday school teacher. Yvonne describes it as like a black cloud hanging over her.

Years later, she received deliverance prayer with regards to the spiritualism, and the black cloud lifted. She wrote to her family explaining her Christian faith, but this only brought exclusion and she became the 'black sheep of the family'. The relationship with her parents was affected by this for ten years. When both her children rebelled and her church blamed her, Yvonne felt great anger, but God began to heal her. Not only that, but she began to develop a prayer ministry enabling others to be free of hurts from the past too. I knew nothing of their story when Yvonne came to me a few years ago to tell me that God was leading them to move to Salford from Didcot to be a part of our church.

God had told them they were to join LCC to be 'grandparents' in the church. This was exactly what we desperately needed. The sacrifice this amazing couple made in relocating, and belonging to a church where there was no one else within twenty years of their age, and simply serving and loving people, is remarkable and wonderful. It is an expression of the kingdom of God in all its beauty. They have nurtured and loved lots of our younger people for many years and seen them develop into mature Christians who now serve and mentor others.

Eight years on, as Yvonne battles cancer, they continue to be an example to all and provide the church with a stability and safety that comes from their years of experience and wisdom. Henri Nouwen wrote a great book called *The Wounded Healer*,[10] exploring the way our wounds can bring healing to others. Martin and Yvonne are great examples of this, using their own experiences, past and present, to bring healing to others. We don't need to wait until we are sorted out till we minister to people. We are all a work in progress, and it is often our own vulnerability that can bring the greatest healing to other people.

One of Martin and Yvonne's small group is called Steph. Steph grew up in Langworthy, started attending some of our Eden Salford events and made a decision to follow Jesus when she was thirteen at a World Wide Message Tribe event. She came to our first-ever LCC meal back in 2004, and has been a part of our community ever since. When Steph was twenty, her mum died, and within two years she had lost her dad too. She began to wonder

---

[10] Henri Nouwen, *The Wounded Healer: Ministry in Contemporary Society* (Darton, Longman & Todd, 2014).

whether God loved her and what the point of life was, but the sense of family at church drew her in. She began to help with a healing rooms ministry and, one week, as she was praying for healing for others, she saw a vision of an angel in white, with her parents standing on either side of it. The angel told her not to worry, and she was filled with peace at the knowledge that her parents were safe with God.

This experience led to Steph getting baptised at an emotional service in 2010, and her experience of God healing her through the toughest possible times was an incredible shining witness to all present. Steph is now a trustee of our LifeCentre charity, and is a key part of all we do at church. What I love about her story is that her healing came when she was bringing healing to others – another wounded healer!

I could go on to tell you many more stories like this. As I was feeling a couple of years ago that God was calling us as a church to a new movement of prayer, especially for children and young people, a friend of mine called Anna called me from Reading to tell me she might fancy coming to visit. She visited for a few weeks and has been here ever since! She is very gifted and experienced in pretty much all the stuff we felt God calling us to do. And she is a brilliant, faithful friend too. This is just as much a miracle as God providing finance, or bringing healing to someone.

My friends Pete and Rachel joined the church a year or two after we started, just as we needed someone to lead us in worship. Not only are they both great worship leaders, but super-talented in many other ways too, bringing leadership and an incredible heart for people and the community. They are another miracle of provision. I could tell you about Barry and Becca who were with us for many years, faithfully living out true missional community, whom I met in a local gym just after they had moved into the area. Barry told me that they were looking for a church they could walk to from their new house. I asked where they lived and he said, 'Langworthy.' It was pretty sure this was another miracle, even though I had hidden my excitement by trying to put them off by telling them about the other churches. Barry told me this only made him want to come to us more! I am often on the lookout for these God-moments.

Often these God-moments seem like accidents. My brother's wife, Natalie, is a key leader in our church, incredibly creative and full of ideas. She originally came to Greater Manchester from Croydon to be a dancer in a Message band, but the band didn't get started and she ended up being given a job working in schools with the Eden Salford team, while she waited for the band to happen. It didn't and instead she started dancing with the Tribe, fell in love with her fellow schools worker (Ar Kid) and ended up helping us to plant the church. I love 'accidents' like that!

God also provides us with friends who don't know Jesus. When Jesus sent out the seventy-two disciples on mission in Luke 10, He told them that when they entered a town they should find a 'person of peace' (CSB) who would welcome them and let them stay at their house. This would be a sign that they should stay in the town and preach the gospel there, accepting their hospitality and healing the sick. I believe that God provides us with such people of peace whenever He calls us to a new place, whether it be an estate such as Langworthy, a workplace, or a people group. We need to have our spiritual eyes open to recognise them.

We found a few people of peace in the local community activists. They were already there, creating community, working for justice, bringing hope, even though most had no Christian faith. I could see that God was at work in and through them anyway! As we worked together we found much in common. Two friends in particular, Lorna and Andy, were both heavily involved in community leadership in the estate, serving people and seeing change happen. Although they did not share our faith, we all wanted to see positive change and a fresh start for our community, and they were very kind in welcoming us and working with us over the years.

When Andy and Lorna left a couple of years ago, we asked them what they had thought of us, and what we could now do for the estate moving forward. They explained how, with all the benefit cuts, the estate was beginning to feel more divided, and what Langworthy really needed was to come together more, to find places where people would not be judged but loved for who they were. One of the ways they said we could help was by getting more people to come to our church, as that was a place they had seen was non-judgemental and could offer a glimpse of hope for people! Andy said that he felt we were living out an example of what Jesus would have done if He had lived in Langworthy. I was taken aback by this and told them that would have been exactly what we would have wanted them to say if I'd written them a script!

I also felt that they had lived the way of Jesus too. They were truly people of peace for us.

Friendships are hugely important in the kingdom of God. I hate the phrase 'friendship evangelism' because it sounds as if you are making friends with someone just so you can evangelise them. We should make friends because Jesus calls us to love people, whether or not they are interested in our faith. It is my view that God is at work in everyone's life, and my job is to spot that and encourage it, whether the person identifies themselves as Christian or not.

A new phase for our friendships in Langworthy has been as many in the church have got married and started families. Often when I tell our stories at churches around the UK, one of the common questions I get is about our kids. 'How do you look after your kids, living in such a difficult area?' 'What about local schools? How do you ensure your kids get a good education?' People are often quite concerned for our children's futures!

Esther and I have three brilliant children – Daniel, Rebekah and Hannah. My hope for them is that, instead of being wrapped in cotton wool to try to protect them from the big bad world, with all its poverty and crime, they would grow up with friendships across all kinds of social divides when it comes to class, ethnicity, affluence/poverty etc. I hope they will develop a heart to love people no matter who they are or where they come from, what colour their skin is or what kind of house they live in. I hope they will grow up to stand for justice in the world and to be able to know and feel how Jesus feels about the world in all its wonder and terror.

Many years ago my brother was running a seminar about Eden at the Spring Harvest conference in Skegness. We were in our early twenties at the time. One concerned older lady asked the question, 'What do your parents think about you all moving into such a dangerous place?' Our parents happened to be in the seminar at the time so Andrew got my mum to come up and answer the question. She thought for a moment and said, 'Well, when it comes down to it, they have to obey what God tells them to do, and if they die, they'll be in heaven with Jesus!' The whole room erupted in laughter, and I said, 'Thanks a lot, Mum!'

But she meant it. We have to obey Jesus, wherever He calls us. And if He calls us, it is as a family, not as individuals. I hope I can trust my children into God's hands just as my mum does. Also, if the local schools are not good enough for our children, they are not good enough for anyone's children, and therefore we need to do something about it. Five people in our small church are local school governors, because we are passionate about seeing children thrive in our community. We are convinced that this estate can be and should be a good place to bring up our children, and that we can help to make that a reality.

As a church we pray for the local schools, and as I write, each one of them is a great place for children to learn, despite the many social issues in our community. The teachers are hugely committed and often go way beyond the call of duty. Our children are growing up meeting people from all kinds of backgrounds, learning to love and understand people who have had much more chaotic lives than them. I am happy about this and I am convinced that my children will be a positive influence for good as they progress through school.

When I lived in Watford I was standing at the front of church preaching about evangelism, when I had a thought. 'I don't actually know anyone in Watford who isn't a Christian, and I'm up here telling hundreds of people they should reach out and tell everyone about Jesus!' I had allowed myself to live in a Christian bubble, which was totally my own fault and not that of the church, but I was ashamed of my hypocrisy and promised God I would never allow that to happen again. I would want to help my children not to fall into that trap either.

A final aspect of friendship for us has been friendship with other churches. Naturally when a new church starts in an area, there is an element of distrust and caution among the existing churches. As well as the man who referred to us as 'the enemy', there was another lady who went round telling people we were a cult. Someone spread a rumour we were brainwashing people by playing Christian music in our youth drop-in! After a couple of years we began to earn trust in the area as we served the other churches and joined in with their events and with inter-church gatherings. Being a small church meant that we lacked the experience of worshipping in a larger gathering, so a few times a year we link up with a nearby Elim church and join them to worship. They have been a real help to us in terms of advice, pastoral help and generosity when we have been in need.

Last year we started a regular worship and prayer gathering attended by people from six or more local churches, culminating in a twenty-four-hour worship and prayer event on New Year's Day when fourteen churches were involved. Coming together to pray is a great way of expressing our unity. For the last few years we have been a part of Party in the Park, a free event attracting 3,000 plus people from the community for fun activities, music and preaching. Joint mission events such as these are a great way of showing the community that the churches are for them and also are not concerned with building their own empires, but with blessing the city.

As well as these more evangelical events, we also work with the local liturgical churches, especially at Easter when we do a Walk of Witness carrying a cross around Salford precinct. This is great for our people who have little experience of the historical richness and rootedness of the ancient Church traditions. It can also lead to amusing experiences, such as one year when we solemnly processed past a man urinating at a bus stop. He looked over his shoulder and said to his mate, 'Ee-ar, what are those lot doing carrying a massive cross around the precinct?' I was more concerned with why he was doing a wee in a bus shelter. We also put on an annual community carol service in the local park where three schools and a number of churches sing carols and hear about the Christmas story as the sun goes down over Langworthy.

Friendship and trust between local churches is hugely important. People from a number of different churches volunteer for our outreach programmes, and we look to work together whenever we can. The more we come together, the more we see Jesus' prayer for us answered: 'I pray also for those who will believe in me through their message, that all of them may be one, Father … May they be brought to complete unity to let the world know that you sent me and have loved them even as you have loved me' (John 17:20-23). I am desperate for the world to know Jesus' love, aren't you? Part of that is the demand that we are in unity with our brothers and sisters from other churches, no matter what our differences are.

To conclude this chapter on friendship, the other type of friendship that has nurtured me over these years is the lifelong friendship with people who have no direct involvement with our work in Langworthy, who are more interested in making me laugh or having a drink with me than how my Alpha course is going: the kind of friendships where you don't see each other for months, but then it's as though you've never been apart, and you laugh so hard you actually think you're going to die, and you end up staying up ridiculously late even though the kids will wake you up at 7am, because you so want to savour this moment. Make sure you don't lose those friendships in the busyness of life, with people who have no agenda with you except to be your friend. Text them, call them, book in time to visit them. They will remind you that life still goes on, even though everything seems to be falling apart.

These life-giving friendships will nurture your soul and give you perspective. They help you to reconnect with the God who just loves you for who you are, not for what you can give Him. God gives us all these different types of friendships in order to grow us. We become mature and get an insight into God's character – the God who welcomes us back when we let Him down, the God who brings us joy, the God who works alongside us in our mission, the God who loves and reaches out to the poor and marginalised, who will never leave us and will never let us down.

You see, at the heart of all the friendships we have is the mind-blowing, world-shaking truth that we get to be friends with God! Abraham 'was called a friend of God' (James 2:23, ESV), and now Jesus makes a way for all of us to experience the wonder of friendship with God! 'I no longer call you servants ... Instead, I have called you friends' (John 15:15). Jesus gives us friends, but more than that, and however undeserving we may feel, the Son of God calls us friends!

Chapter 10
A Week in Langworthy

I want to conclude by giving you a virtual tour of a typical week in Langworthy. Imagine you have come to visit us for a week to get a feel for what we do. You arrive on a Saturday night to make sure you are not late for church in the morning, only to discover that we don't meet until 12.30pm. The unexpected bonus of a lie-in gives you a good start to the week! Around midday on Sunday, you set off with your hosts to walk to church. On your way you notice the rows of red-brick terraced houses, interspersed with grassy areas where blocks have been knocked down but nothing built in their place. There are children playing in the street, and they all run out of the way as a raucous motorbike speeds past doing a wheelie. You pass numerous takeaways, beauty salons and betting shops, and a pile of black bin bags spilling out litter on to the road. As you pass the Polish shop you look across the main road to see people coming out of the Anglican/Methodist church after their service, and hear the thumping music of the Pentecostal church meeting above the carpet shop.

As you arrive at Willow Tree school, you are struck by the bright colours of the building and notice that the car park is almost empty. This is because everyone who comes to LCC lives within walking distance of each other. I greet you at the door and make some typical church leader remark about many of our people being away this week, and we walk into the hall together. You instantly think, 'Wow, there are a lot of kids! And they are quite loud!' As you look round the hall there are people sitting around tables, music playing and people in the kitchen preparing food. You notice that one side of the hall is one huge window, making the room light and vibrant but also giving a view of the terraced houses and, beyond that, the tower blocks of Salford precinct. This reminds our church that we are not here to escape from the outside world, but to be equipped to be sent back out to change it for the better.

You sit at a table and I introduce you to Sharon and Craig and their family, who have been coming along for a few years now. Sharon and I went to the same school in Salford, and she tells you some of her story, the bereavements she has suffered and the struggles that has produced, but also how her life is being changed by Jesus. Sharon is very kind and friendly and instantly helps you to feel at home. Craig has started coming along more recently than Sharon, but is already serving by helping with the PA set-up and is finding a connection with God too. He recently told me of the peace and comfort he has found and his appreciation of how down to earth everyone is, and how he loves and shares our heart for the community.

I stand at the front and welcome everyone, explaining that it is our monthly Worship Sunday, which means that after our food, the adults will all go out to another room for their session, to sing and have a talk and pray. As you eat, the hall is buzzing with conversation, laughter and young children playing. We go up the stairs for the adults' session. You are surprised how few people are left after all the children's workers have been taken out! We sing together, and you notice that some people don't know all the songs. Others raise their hands and sing loudly. There are moments of quiet where prophetic words are given, and then there is a twenty-minute talk, followed by a response where people receive prayer ministry. The lady next to you is crying gently, and you put your hand on her shoulder to pray for her. You later discover it is her first time too. Her daughter had met us through the school's work and dragged her mum along, and here she is, meeting with God.

You enjoyed yourself, but it all seemed rather small and unimpressive. Slightly disappointed, you say to me, 'Is that it?' I say, 'No, that's just a small part of it. That's our family meal. The rest of the week will show you what we're all about.'

Afterwards you come with us to the park to play a game called Kubb, a Viking game which involves throwing wooden blocks around. Children from the local schools recognise some of us and join in, and bring their parents to play too. Afterwards I take you down to the bottom of Langworthy Road, where the estate ends and MediaCityUK begins. The BBC have moved much of their programming here, and ITV are prominent too. We look round the *Blue Peter* garden and pop into one of the cool bars. We are a five-minute walk from Langworthy but it feels like another world.

Monday

It's an early start today as you are helping out at our Breakfast Group. Every morning in term time, up to ten children (referred by the school) come to have breakfast at LifeCentre. The places are free and the focus of the group is to develop the children's understanding of their feelings, ability to make friends and start the school day in a calm way, ready to learn. All of them are from backgrounds where home life is difficult, but all have improved their attendance and punctuality, and three-quarters have improved their academic performance against expectations after joining the group. Kerry, our Northern Irish legend, welcomes you as you come in. Kerry is in her final year of Bible college and is passionate about social justice, and is one of our main youth and kids' workers. At first the children look at you suspiciously, but by the end of the session they are all asking you if you want to come back tomorrow! You also enjoy the family atmosphere – a rowdy family, but family anyway.

After Breakfast Group you have a break before Alpha starts at lunchtime. As you help to prepare the food for Alpha, you reflect on the fact that you have been to three events so far, and all have been around tables involving food! This is no accident. You see a poster on the wall in the LifeCentre advertising our upcoming Make Lunch sessions in the school holidays – hot food and fun activities throughout the holidays, especially aimed at the children who may not get a nutritious hot meal otherwise. Holiday hunger is a serious issue for many families here. We deliver the sessions in the local schools for up to forty children each day, three days a week. In Jesus' kingdom, all are welcome to the table, especially those who are hungry.

The group arrive for Alpha. There is food, then a short talk followed by discussion. During the food you get to know Sloane, a mother of seven, who has been on a journey back to God during the last year or two. From a family with a Muslim dad and Christian mum, she experienced a violent and sometimes confusing religious upbringing. Her dad left her mum for another woman on Sloane's ninth birthday. She had her first child at seventeen, and fell into a cycle of drug and alcohol abuse and daily violence from her boyfriend. She ended up homeless for a while, struggling with mental health, suicidal thoughts and self-harm.

With a new man, Sloane's family eventually expanded to seven children. During this period, Sloane discovered the father of her first child dead, experienced the father of her other children leaving then returning on several occasions, and then the tragic death of a premature baby. At that point she decided there was no God, and started with drink and drugs again. Then she was diagnosed with cervical cancer twice, and was convinced she was going to die, but somehow survived.

She was invited to an LCC Christmas meal a couple of years ago, and felt welcomed and accepted. The church was there for her as her marriage broke down, and recently we had the honour of leading a dedication service for six of her children. I asked Sloane what this meant to her, and she said, 'This is about my family being welcomed into the church.' It was our privilege to do so, and was a wonderful and emotional occasion. Sloane has found her faith coming alive, and has found healing and comfort from the Bible, the worship and the experience of a non-judgemental community. She describes herself as a sheep who was lost but is now found.

More recently Sloane has begun to use her music in the church, playing some songs as we took communion in a recent service. We discovered that she had been part of a church music group as a child, and brought along her old Spring Harvest music book from the 1990s! I had to smile when I thought of the fact that she was leading our worship that day with a tattoo on her arm that says 'Still I rise', followed by a seriously obscene word plain for all to see! It reminded me of the lady in Luke 7:36-50 who has had a difficult past. She comes to worship Jesus and washes His feet, and Jesus loves and welcomes her worship while others look on in judgement. This is the amazing grace of God.

The group discussion is lively and often hilarious. People say whatever they think without holding back, but there is a seriousness underlying it all, and a genuine desire to learn and to know Jesus. Once or twice there are 'holy moments' when we are all aware of the presence of God among us. Some go quiet, others feel tingly or emotional. We always end with prayer and listening to God. Some who have never prophesied before have a go, even if they don't call themselves Christians yet. One lady reports having felt peace for the first time in years.

You end up chatting to Lisa while you tidy up at the end. Lisa is Sloane's friend who is currently ahead of Sloane in the 'how many kids' count, with eight! Lisa is very funny and incredibly helpful and kind. Before Lisa came regularly to church, Sloane had persuaded her to come to our weekend away. When Sloane pulled out at the last minute, Lisa bravely decided to still come without her, not really knowing anyone, and dreading that she would hate it. In the end, she had a great time and established herself in the church, rather than just being 'Sloane's friend'. She is on a journey of discovering who Jesus is, but already we can't imagine our church without her and her brilliant family. She has told us since she has joined that her confidence has bloomed, she is starting to understand the story of the Bible and she has made lots of friends. We are glad to be her friends.

Straight after Alpha is our Transition Group, helping Year 6 kids with the big and scary step up to high school.

In the evening you meet up with our team on the Eden Bus near Salford precinct. There had been months of trouble with local youngsters damaging property and other types of antisocial behaviour in the area, but since the bus started coming, it has gone really quiet. Not only are there no incidents on the actual night the team are there, but all the other nights have seen a huge drop in trouble and the kids have started playing together rather than causing mischief. The police are delighted and have helped to fund the project.

Tuesday

We worked you hard yesterday, but you did want to see everything! We meet in the LifeCentre prayer room at 9.30am for our twice-weekly morning prayers. We read the Scriptures together and pray for the church and our community, and any specific requests we have been given.

Then you rush over to a local primary school to see an RE lesson my brother is delivering about how the Bible was written.

In the afternoon, as it is the summer term, you come along to our community course that we are running for Year 3 children. This annual course that we run in two primary schools helps the children learn about who lives in their community, who to contact when in need, and mostly, how they can make a difference in the community. This week we have the local community police officer coming in, to remind the children that the police are there to help them and are not a threat to them. One child asks the PC if it was her who arrested his brother! In the second half of the session, an older lady comes in to tell the kids what Langworthy was like during the war. They are spellbound as she tells them one story after another, including her testimony of how she came to faith along the way!

A lady who had worked in Manchester schools transferred to Salford a few years ago. She said the big difference she had noticed in our area is that the children's aspirations are lower, and they lack hope. I was stunned by this and we see this community course as one way of raising aspirations, and bringing hope that change can happen.

In the evening you attend Rachel's fitness class for local women. Rachel has this vision to see the health of Langworthy completely turned around for the better over the next few years, and her fitness classes and running groups are just the start for her. It's the kind of crazy idea that might just happen, and Rachel is the kind of person who is ideal to see it through!

Wednesday

Today you turn up to LifeCentre to help with our Food Parcels project in partnership with the Red Cross. Esther runs this with Yvonne and her son, Pete. Ten to fifteen parcels are given out each week to destitute asylum seekers – mostly people with no access to any benefits who are not allowed to get a job. As well as the food, they are offered essentials such as razors and soap, and sometimes help with filling in forms and other vital advice. Some of these people were in high-flying jobs in their home countries, but now are reduced to brokenness and desperation from the trauma of having to flee their country and the lack of welcome they have found here. We hope to offer them some taster of the kindness and hospitality of Jesus.

At lunchtime we go to the Salford Leaders' Lunch where sixty leaders from across the city gather together to worship and pray for one another, and share about the latest initiatives the churches are pioneering for their communities.

In the evening you go along to Martin and Yvonne's small group for some Bible teaching and prayer. The group have had many years together learning from Martin's Bible knowledge and hearing God for each other. You are massively encouraged when they spend time listening for prophetic words for you, and leave feeling uplifted and challenged.

Thursday

After morning prayers, we stick around at LifeCentre and welcome those coming for our free counselling services and the monthly free legal advice clinic. Later on, you go to more lessons with my brother and he tells you about the mentoring services he provides for the schools too.

We have a walk round the estate, observing the redevelopment of some terraced blocks into modern 'upside down' houses, with the bedrooms on the ground floor and communal areas at the back, that have attracted young professionals into the area. We walk past a community centre called the Cornerstone that provides vital services for local people in need. Owing to his work in the schools over many years, and his personality, most people seem to know Andrew as we walk around the streets. A young man shouts across the road, 'Andy, you muppet!' This is meant affectionately, you are assured by Andrew. The guy used to come to one of his high school lunch clubs.

Friday

Today you start off with an assembly in front of 400 children. We teach them a Christian song, and give them a talk from the Bible. By this stage many of the kids remember you and you feel rather popular as they wave at you and call your name as they leave the assembly. Next we go off to another leaders' prayer gathering, and you finish the day in a last RE lesson in school. In the evening we take you to the 'curry mile' in Manchester to sample the finest Indian cuisine for miles around.

Saturday

We try our hardest to not organise events on a Saturday, as we value the principle of Sabbath and want our people to rest. But there is a group that happens in LifeCentre for more than twenty people, mostly Iranians, consisting of Bible study and learning English, ending with – you've guessed it – a meal for all who attended.

Sunday

On your last day with us we are back at Willow Tree school at 12.30pm. This Sunday is called The Big Eat, when we invite people from all the projects we are involved with to join us for food and storytelling. The room is packed full and our core people have their work cut out trying to greet people and make sure everyone feels welcome. Rachel tells us about a lady she prayed for at her fitness group who had injured her wrist, and it was healed when she prayed. The Breakfast Group children have come, some with their parents, and they give us an insight into what goes on each morning in their group. We pray for them while they stand with us at the front. A local musician who we got to know through our live music evenings comes up and performs a couple of his songs. He isn't a Christian, but feels as much part of this as anyone else. It is loud and fairly chaotic, but fun, hospitable and sometimes beautiful.

You have reached the end of your visit and I drive you over to the station to get your train home. What I hope you have understood during this week is that the church is not just about Sundays. When you said, 'Is that it?', you hit the nail on the head. No, that most definitely is not it. It is a daily thing, expressed through meetings on Sundays, but also through all that you've seen this week, and a whole bunch of things you haven't seen. It's expressed through my mate Pete who works at the university, and Susan, who is a midwife. It is expressed through the mums at local toddler groups, and Beth at the school governors' meeting. Whether we are gathered or scattered, we are church. Church happens when Lisa looks after Sloane's kids as well as her own eight when Sloane has to go to hospital. It happens when our children are recognised by their teachers for being particularly kind and helpful to others. Is that it? No, there is all this and loads more.

Conclusion

I want to end this book by reflecting once more on Jesus' meal table. At the start of our adventure in church planting, we had a dream of a church that was incredibly accessible to all, inclusive and welcoming, and at the same time believed in the power of the gospel to change lives and pursued an experience of the Holy Spirit that brought about healing and other miracles. And all of this would be built on a long-term commitment to a specific, small geographical area centred around Langworthy. We wanted community transformation, and knew that would not be possible without individuals being transformed by Jesus. We have tried to work well with all the secular agencies, and at the same time we have worked to form a countercultural community (the church) centred around Jesus, to give people a glimpse of the kingdom of God. This remains our dream, at the same time as we are seeing some of it become a reality.

It has been much slower then we first imagined. It has been smaller, and less impressive than our original grandiose visions. But looking back, I do think we have been *faithful* to what God has called us to do. Has it been a success? I was tempted to call this book *Success and How to Avoid It: A Story of Church Planting in the Inner City.* In all seriousness, though, the success is always in obedience, not in numbers or prominence.

Jesus' habit of table fellowship with sinners caused a scandal in His day. But it was at the heart of His message about the kingdom of God. This is not just a side issue, but absolutely central to His message. The prostitutes are coming into the kingdom ahead of the Pharisees! There is a woe for the rich and a blessing for the poor! The sinful woman was allowed to kiss His feet and anoint Him with perfume to express her worship to Him, and she would be an example to all generations who would follow wherever the gospel is preached! This woman was a worship leader for us all. She was a known sinner – probably a prostitute – and one of our greatest worship leaders. Her story, and Jesus' affirmation of her worship, was preserved by the earliest Church, even though it would have been an embarrassing story. This is how we should be! Our task is to bring people to Jesus so they can worship Him too, and find healing in the process.

Sadly, the communal meals started by Jesus did not last long in the early Church, ultimately being banned by Augustine in the fourth century, but by that stage they had long become detached from the sacraments and largely lost their purpose. Perhaps in our day, the common meal of Jesus can be revived? The physical act of sitting round a table and eating together, in the presence of Jesus, with the clear expectation of meeting Jesus as we eat together? And for those meals to be inclusive of all, no matter what our background? If our churches are neat and tidy and everyone looks the same and is on their best behaviour, perhaps we can begin to consider this as a major problem?

When Pete Greig wrote his Vision in that first 24–7 prayer room, he said, 'Herald the weirdos! Summon the losers and the freaks. Here come the frightened and forgotten with fire in their eyes.' Do we say 'amen' to that? Or perhaps, 'Yes, that would be good, but not too many weirdos or freaks, please!' It seems to me that this is what Jesus' table looked like. Not the kind of people you would invite to your cheese and wine party. Are we followers of Jesus or not? We long for the power that Jesus experienced to be seen in our own lives – to heal the sick, cast out demons and see lives transformed as He did. But we would rather not invite all those disreputable people to share our lives, and disturb our comfort. We would much rather give money to charities so they can do that for us! We would rather not fast and pray as He did, for forty days in the desert, and we would quite like to ignore His promise that 'In this world you will have trouble' (John 16:33).

The apostle Paul put those two things together in his letter to the Philippians: 'I want to know Christ and the power of his resurrection and the fellowship of sharing in his sufferings' (Philippians 3:10). If we want to experience His power, we must be willing to suffer too. Imagine if a whole generation of Christians put their ambitions and desires for greatness to one side and just went after Jesus instead. If we just rejected the world's ideas of success, and tried to imitate Jesus. I was at a conference only the other day when someone said something like, 'I can't get away from the idea that I was born for greatness' – to whoops and 'amens' from the large crowd. I will say 'amen' to that, if we use Jesus' definition of greatness – a life of washing feet and taking the lowest place and serving those who nobody else wants to touch. We must be followers of Jesus.

As we come to the end of this book, what are our hopes and dreams for the future? I dream of Isaiah's vision coming to pass in Langworthy:

> The desert and the parched land will be glad;
> the wilderness will rejoice and blossom.
> Like the crocus, it will burst into bloom;
> it will rejoice greatly and shout for joy.
> The glory of Lebanon will be given to it,
> the splendour of Carmel and Sharon;
> they will see the glory of the LORD,
> the splendour of our God.
>
> Strengthen the feeble hands,
> steady the knees that give way;
> say to those with fearful hearts,
> 'Be strong, do not fear;
> your God will come,
> he will come with vengeance;
> with divine retribution
> he will come to save you.'
>
> Then will the eyes of the blind be opened
> and the ears of the deaf unstopped.
> Then will the lame leap like a deer,
> and the mute tongue shout for joy.
> Water will gush forth in the wilderness
> and streams in the desert.
> *Isaiah 35:1-6*

I dream of a time when all children in our estate can grow up in safety, and there would be no need for our nurture groups or counselling services. In the meantime, I hope and pray for a generation to rise up and not to be restricted by what has gone before – by generational unemployment, by alcoholism and other addictions, by the temptation of a life of crime, or by lack of hope and aspirations. I pray that God would pour out His Spirit in such a way as to break those curses over so many of the children in our estate. We have prayed for years for whole households to be saved, not just one from one family and two from another. We are beginning to see this happen at the moment. God hears our prayers.

We are praying and believing that the health of our estate and of our whole city will change dramatically for the better over the next few years. We are praying that the healings and miracles I have described in this book are only a tiny glimpse of what is to come. We have seen incredible partnerships with our local schools develop, and we hope we can continue and grow them, and be worthy of the trust we have earned. We long for more of our friends who are coming to faith to develop into leaders within the Church and community.

But I guess, most of all, we pray that God would continue to give us the grace to keep plodding on. Giving us eyes to see and celebrate the ordinary miracles that He is bringing about day by day, month by month, year by year. Helping us to just love the next person we meet, and to persevere when things get tough and people let us down. To give us the courage not to leave when it feels as if things are falling apart, and the courage to have hope when it is easier to give it up.

Recently I was on a retreat on Holy Island and went into the church on the island to pray. There were two signs telling the stories of the great saints of the island, Cuthbert and Aidan. At the bottom of Cuthbert's story it said in large letters 'Cuthbert, Fire of the North'. This was a man of prayer who saw many miracles in his life and yet was rooted in a small geographical area. I prayed that we would see that kind of fire in Langworthy, and that my own life might be a Fire of the North, but over to the north-west!

Then I read Aidan's story, the man who came over from Iona to bring the Christian gospel to the stubborn tribes of the north of England. Like his later successor, Cuthbert, Aidan was based on Holy Island. Aidan built schools and hospitals as well as churches. A humble man with little regard for possessions, he always travelled on foot rather than horseback, and talked with and listened to the people. He saw many people come to faith. At the end of his story, he was summarised as 'a good man who in his day pleased God'. I thought about this and decided that would be good enough for me. Not going after greatness but goodness, not listing successes and numbers, just the wonderful truth that 'in his day, he pleased God'. That is my prayer for our work going forward, that we would always live to be good people who please God.